Photograph contributed by a member of the 2-127th

Private Soldiers

Joseph Streeter

Private Soldiers

A Year in Iraq
with a Wisconsin National Guard Unit

Benjamin Buchholz

Photographs by Joseph Streeter and Nathan Olson

Afterword by Brigadier General Charles J. Barr

Wisconsin Historical Society Press

Published by the

Wisconsin Historical Society Press

Publication of this book was made possible in part by gifts from Chester L. Krause, Douglas and Myrtle Ogilvie, and Robert F. Froehlke.

All royalties from sales of *Private Soldiers* will go to the 2-127th's family support groups and to funds established in memoriam of the battalion members who gave their lives in the Iraq War.

Printed in the United States of America
Designed by Kay Wimberly and Becky Leclair of The AVS Group, Inc.

11 10 09 08 07   1 2 3 4 5

Buchholz, Benjamin.
Private soldiers : a year in Iraq with a Wisconsin National Guard Unit / Benjamin Buchholz ;
photographs by Joseph Streeter and Nathan Olson.—1st ed.
p. cm.
Includes index.
ISBN 978-0-87020-395-4 (hardcover : alk. paper)
1. Iraq War, 2003—Personal narratives, American.
2. Wisconsin. National Guard—History—21st century. I. Streeter, Joseph. II. Olson, Nathan. III. Title.
DS79.76.B82 2007
956.7044'342—dc22
2007011306

In memory of Andrew Wallace, Michael Wendling, Ryan Jopek,
and all those who have given their lives in war to preserve the ideal of democracy.

Nathan Olson

Contents

Benjamin Buchholz

Introduction

In February 2006, sitting on my bunk in a tent where I lived with five other men, I settled down to one of the best moments in a deployed soldier's life. I'd just received a care package from my wife. I began to imagine what would be inside . . . Wisconsin cheese, DVDs, notes from home, pictures of my two young children, maybe a snowball packed in dry ice?

Most striking of everything tucked away in that box, I unwrapped a little white and green clay pot of the type kindergartners excel at producing. My five-year-old son's fingerprints were hardened on the rim. I set it on the desk beside my bunk, filled it with POGs (fake money) from the PX and other knickknacks, and took a picture of it to send home to him: "See, daddy's using your dish."

Something interesting happened when I snapped that picture. I caught, in the background, other knickknacks, things I'd collected during my work in Iraq, things I'd saved from previous care packages, things I'd brought back with me from mid-tour leave, other ubiquitous items, like a bottle of Rawdatain water. The picture made me think about living crammed together with grown men in a tent eight time zones away from my family. It made me wonder how much I had been changed by the experience of being deployed.

And I realized that all of our soldiers had been changed by this deployment and the separation from their homes and families. I began to interview guys, taking photos of their living areas. I wanted to document what it was like when our mess hall, in the desert, flooded; how it felt to get a haircut and backrub from the contracted Indian barbers; what the weight room and coffee shop were like on post; and how similar this war and past wars were even though we had email, webcams in our tents, and banks of phones easy to access in the Morale, Welfare, and Recreation tent.

That was the project's genesis. It greatly expanded and improved in quality when I added the skills of two professional photographers, First Lieutenant Nathan Olson and Staff Sergeant Joseph Streeter, who also deployed with us. They carried their own expensive cameras around Iraq with them on missions, sometimes holding a .50cal gun in one hand while propping their camera in the crook of their other arm. That view from the turret of the Humvee provides this project something that few other books can boast: a direct view from the level of those who led missions and participated in all facets of the deployment.

Drawn from the Red Arrow 32nd Infantry Brigade, our unit, the 2-127th Gator Battalion, was based out of Camp Navistar, Kuwait. The 32nd Infantry is the largest unit in the Wisconsin National Guard, with about 3,600 of the state's 7,700 soldiers. The National Guard, unlike the active Army, has not deployed in large numbers to minor conflicts, although some units have gone in the past to Bosnia, Panama, and elsewhere. The 32nd Brigade had not been deployed overseas since World War II. So the call-up of the Guard all across the nation in support of Operation Iraqi Freedom was a definite milestone, signaling a shift in national thinking from using the Guard as a strategic reserve to employing it as an operationally ready and relevant force. But that operational readiness does not come without drawbacks and limitations: We are citizen soldiers. We have civilian jobs and families unaccustomed to long periods of separation. Some of us are students trying to finish college. In these things we find challenges unique to the Reserves (the National Guard and the federal Reserves), but we also find a great source of strength—active duty forces do not get the same sort of hometown support, nor do they bring with them anywhere near the variety of professional skills and abilities we found so useful in completing our mission: carpenters, plumbers, electricians, lawyers, schoolteachers, and—yes—photographers.

The soldiers in the 2-127th came from all over Wisconsin and included representation from other states interspersed in companies headquartered in Appleton, Green Bay, Fond du Lac, Waupun/Ripon, and Merrill/Antigo. We provided armed escort for convoys of up to fifty civilian-contracted and military semis throughout all of Iraq, from Umm Qasr in the south to Mosul in the far north. It was a lonely mission, with three up-armored Humvees operating independently to shepherd each convoy to bases far from our headquarters. This independence required enormous maturity, responsibility, and tactical know-how from junior soldiers.

We fielded three regular infantry companies in our battalion, each deployed in a non-standard infantry configuration with twenty-four Humvee teams of three soldiers each. Each infantry company also provided supply and administrative support. The headquarters company for the battalion, with three Humvee teams of its own, added another layer of support along with specialty staff to keep abreast of intelligence, operational planning, and soldier welfare during the fight. In total we had 620 soldiers and around 150 Humvees on the road or working to support the road crews, day and night.

From May 2005, when we mobilized for training at Camp Shelby, Mississippi, through our homecoming in August 2006, with a brief respite for mid-tour leave for each of us sometime between October 2005 and June 2006, the soldiers of the 2-127th Infantry Battalion served in Operation Iraqi Freedom. Nathan, Joe, and I have done what we can to document how soldiers lived, how we performed our unique mission, how we trained, and how we bonded as a unit. Those bonds are difficult to capture on film, more difficult yet to describe in words. The true testament to their strength will come fifty years from now, when we still number among our best friends the men with whom we rode into battle this last year.

—CAPTAIN BENJAMIN BUCHHOLZ
November 27, 2006

ALERT SCRIPT

THE FOLLOWING ALERT SCRIPT WILL BE USED FOR UNITS OF THE 2-127 INFANTRY UPON RECEIPT OF AN ALERT. THE ALERT WILL BE INITIATED BY THE BATTALION COMMANDER, BATTALION EXECUTIVE OFFICER, OR BATTALION S-3.

CALLERS ARE NOT TO ADD ANY INFORMATION TO THIS SCRIPT, ENGAGE IN CONJECTURE OR DISCUSS RUMORS. ADDITIONAL SPECIFIC INFORMATION WILL BE PROVIDED IN FOLLOW-ON MESSAGES ONCE AVAILABLE.

"This is _____ (caller's name and rank).

"I'm calling to notify you that the 2d Battalion, 127th Infantry has received an alert notification. This means the Battalion is expected to be ordered to active duty in the very near future in support of Operation Iraqi Freedom. While a specific timeline is still being developed, we expect to begin a home station mobilization in approximately 30 days. Deployment of the Battalion remains contingent upon receipt of a mobilization order which has not yet been received.

"Upon mobilization, we will be activated for more than one full year in order to perform an overseas mission of an entire year 'boots on the ground.' We expect the total length of the mobilization to be approximately 18 months, however National Guard units may be kept on active duty for as long as 24 months under a Partial Mobilization.

"The National Guard Bureau has given us this notification so that all affected troops, families, and employers can prepare. The information you are being provided in this alert is not for public release, but only for members of your family and your employer. The State Public Affairs office is expected to begin acknowledging the Battalion's alert notification after Soldier notifications have begun. If you receive any questions from the media, they will be directed to State Public Affairs Officer LTC Tim Donovan.

"Effective today _____ (today's date) there will be no transfers or separations from the 2d Battalion, 127th Infantry. This 'Stop Loss' order is authorized by the Director of the Army National Guard in Washington and directed by the Adjutant General of Wisconsin.

"We expect to have more information for you in the near future. You should begin thinking about personal, family and employment arrangements that you will need to make. Once we have received an actual mobilization order, we will contact you again with more specific information.

"Do you understand this notification?

"Do you have any questions at this time?"

QUESTIONS AND ANSWERS

Q. Will I have to go? Is this voluntary?

A. This would be an <u>involuntary</u> activation. Members of the unit would be ordered to active duty with or without their consent.

Q. When will this mobilization take effect?

A. If the alert notification results in an actual mobilization order, the Army's <u>plan</u> is to give you at least 30 days from today (the date of your alert) until your unit receives an actual mobilization order. This is the <u>plan</u>, however the mobilization order could come sooner.

Q. Who can I tell about this? Is this information classified?

A. This notification is not classified, however it is not intended for public release. You may inform your family and employer so they can prepare for your absence.

Q. I am currently enrolled in college and/or plan to enroll for the spring semester. What should I do?

A. Don't do anything now. If the unit is mobilized (as we expect), state and federal law allow you to dis-enroll without penalty.

Q. What about leases?

A. We advise you <u>not</u> to take any actions at this time. If you are ordered to active duty, the law gives you the right to terminate your lease with no penalty.

Q. How long will this mobilization last?

A. Although we expect this mobilization will last approximately 18 months, it is possible that it could last as long as 24 months under the authority of Title 10 U.S. Code (Section 12302), which defines Partial Mobilization.

Q. Is it possible this alert will not result in an actual mobilization order?

A. Yes, it is possible no actual mobilization of your unit will occur, however all soldiers of 2d Battalion, 127th Infantry should make appropriate preparations in anticipation the unit will be mobilized.

Welcome Letter
from Battalion Commander Lieutenant Colonel Todd Taves
and Command Sergeant Major Rafael Conde
April 23, 2005

Welcome to the Family Interactive Website for the 2nd Battalion, 127th Infantry. We hope you will find this site to be a useful tool for both soldiers and their family members to communicate, to share information, and to provide mutual support to one another. This site will also be used by the command to provide general updates to family members as we conduct our movement to Mobilization Station Shelby, and to our eventual destination in the overseas theater of operation. As our situation permits, we will do our best to provide you with the current status of the Battalion and updates on how your soldiers are doing.

The coming weeks will undoubtedly be difficult for family members and soldiers alike as we adjust to new routines, endure separation from our loved ones, and undergo the transition from part-time to full-time members of the military. During this time of adjustment, be assured that your soldiers will receive the very best training and equipment that the Army can provide, and that they will be well taken care of. During our training period at Mobilization Station Shelby, the focus of our activities will be to ensure we have taken all steps necessary to make the unit ready to perform its overseas mission.

As Commander and Command Sergeant Major of the Task Force, we also want to make a special point to welcome to our organization the soliders and family members of Troop E, 105th Calvary, the 32nd Engineer Company, as well as the many individual soldiers and family members from organizations throughout the state that will be part of the Gator Battalion for this deployment. We are proud to have you on board and want to make sure that all of you feel welcomed into your "new" family.

While our family members have always been an important part of our Guard organization, now more than ever our soldiers will be relying on your support as we undertake our assigned mission. We acknowledge and appreciate the many hardships and sacrifices that families will face on the home front and extend our sincere appreciation for all that you do to make it possible for your soldier to serve our nation.

Send-off Remarks
from Battalion Commander Lieutenant Colonel Todd Taves
Given at Camp Douglas, June 5, 2005

Governor Doyle, General Officers, Distinguished Visitors, Friends, Family Members and Soldiers of the Gator Battalion,

Today we are about to embark on a journey to write another page in the proud history of the combat service of the 2nd Battalion 127th Infantry and the Red Arrow Brigade. Those that have gone before us have built that history in places like Antietam, Gettysburg, Meuse-Argonne, New Guinea, Leyte, and Luzon. It is now our responsibility to carry on this proud heritage in the finest tradition of the Wisconsin citizen soldier.

Like those men and women who have gone before us, some of whom are here in our company today, we leave with mixed emotions ranging from pride, excitement, uncertainty, and sadness for the family members and friends who we must now leave behind. While this separation will be difficult, it reminds of us of the necessity to defend this great democracy and strengthens our resolve to accomplish our mission.

Soldiers of the Gator Battalion, you represent the very finest Wisconsin has to offer, and today begins a long journey that will test each one of us in many ways. Many of you have been in the Battalion for years, and others we are welcoming for the first time this week. Through our training in the weeks ahead, we will forge our new team, hone our skills with the training at Camp Shelby, and prepare to execute our assigned missions. Not only will we be successful, but we will also set the standard in professionalism and training for those units with whom we have occasion to work.

As I have watched you prepare for this deployment over the past several weeks, never have I been more impressed by your commitment, professionalism, and sense of purpose. While the challenges we will face together are great, you are clearly up to the task, and I am proud to be in your company.

To our family and friends, you should all be very proud of what your soldiers have already accomplished, and of what they will accomplish. While we will certainly face many challenges in the weeks and months ahead, we know that some of the toughest times will be for those we leave behind. We will do our best to keep you informed as to how your soldiers are doing and what they are experiencing, and rest assured the soldiers will be well trained and taken care of. In our absence please take care of one another and know that we will be thinking of you always.

Thank you all for being here today and the tremendous display of support. Keep us in your prayers as we do the same, and we look forward to the time when we will meet here again to be reunited.

Strike forward and God speed.

Our soldiers board the plane that will take them to Camp Shelby, Mississippi, to train for deployment. Soldiers' families were allowed to come as far as the front edge of the big hangar before parting.

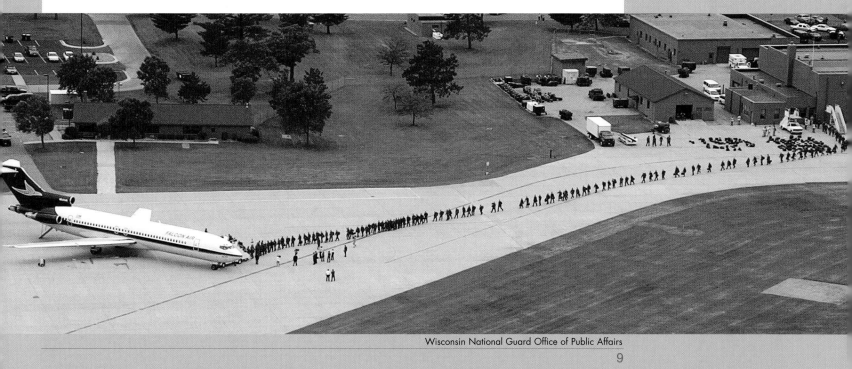

Wisconsin National Guard Office of Public Affairs

9

CHAPTER 1

Training

Training for deployment started long before we were certain we would get the call. Rumors, reports, the state of the world in 2003 and 2004 led us all to expect our unit would soon be activated. Some of our younger soldiers actually enlisted because of the expectation that they'd see battle.

The two years leading up to mobilization included increasingly realistic and refined training: scenarios that incorporated new enemy tactics and greater emphasis on the basic soldiering skills that would be essential no matter what mission we were called upon to perform.

During pre-mobilization training we spent increasing amounts of time on marksmanship, on learning how to use newly fielded communications equipment, and on medical training.

Our families prepared themselves, too, putting important documents in order and taking advantage of programs offered by our state headquarters: legal preparation, family counseling, and the activation of Family Readiness Groups.

Before ever setting foot in the desert we learned a vast amount about the battle being fought in Iraq, and we practiced specific tactics we would later perform as a mounted convoy security element. And perhaps most importantly, bonds of camaraderie were strengthened and forged anew. We learned the expectations of our leaders. And we started the process of becoming lifelong friends—more than friends, as we formed bonds based on continual shared danger and mutual, almost telepathic understanding.

Joseph Streeter

At Camp Shelby soldiers practice entering and clearing room-to-room in a mock house. While training at Shelby we already knew that our mission would not involve room-clearing, but such practice prepared us for the possibility of changing missions midway through the deployment. And it provided an excellent method for working on communication within teams, a valuable skill in convoy operations.

All the training pays off when a team finally hits the road for its first mission. From that point forward teammates rely on each other for almost everything.

Joseph Streeter

We left for Camp Shelby, Mississippi, in June 2005 to begin three months of intensive training. The Wisconsin National Guard staged a farewell ceremony at Volk Field, and several thousand people showed up for a red, white, and blue departure.

Training at Camp Shelby was adequate, if not glorious. At least Mississippi's sweltering heat prepared us northerners a little for the scorching weather of Kuwait and Iraq.

By the time we arrived at Camp Shelby we knew we would perform most of our in-country duty as convoy security escorts. Much of our training now focused on traditional attack and defense, skills we would not use in our overseas mission but that were mandated for all deploying infantry units. For this reason many of our soldiers adopted a "check-the-box" attitude: Get through it, and get to Iraq as soon as possible so the one-year clock could start ticking.

Joseph Streeter

Joseph Streeter

FAR LEFT:
Sergeant Zachary Zuehlsdorf assists one of his squad members as they train on the .50-caliber machine gun.

LEFT:
Sergeant Thad Salverson aims his M4 in the rain while completing the reflex fire training lane.

BELOW:
A soldier sights his close-combat optic around a corner during the room-clearing exercise.

Our training was validated by Camp Shelby's staff, a process in which our unit leadership, along with observer/controller-trainers from Camp Shelby, watched, critiqued, evaluated, and determined when each team, squad, and platoon was proficient in its duties. The main evaluation events included live-fire convoy escort lanes, room clearing, medical training, communication equipment training, and personnel records review. These teams would go to war together and generally spend every minute of their lives for the next year together. Sometimes, though, when missions require it, teams split up. This makes it imperative that every soldier knows how to perform these basic tasks to a standard—allowing them to swap into another team with minimal readjustment.

We began on-the-job training as soon as we reached Kuwait in August 2005. One soldier described stepping off the plane into the Kuwaiti heat this way: Imagine opening an oven when you're making pizza. Stick your head inside, and then have someone turn on a sandblaster so you get the feeling of hot sand and dust pummeling you. During those first weeks of training in Kuwait, our main concerns were hydration and acclimatization, getting our bodies used to 130-degree temperatures.

Joseph Streeter

Joseph Streeter

ABOVE:

The ubiquitous check-mark sign indicates another training task complete—and demonstrates the development of camaraderie through shared suffering.

RIGHT:

Governor Doyle presents a Wisconsin flag to our battalion commander, Lieutenant Colonel Taves, at the Camp Shelby graduation ceremony.

FAR RIGHT:

Our colors at the Relief in Place/Transfer of Authority ceremony. This event marked the official start of our mission and the end of our predecessors' time on the job.

Joseph Streeter   Joseph Streeter

In Kuwait our troops requalified on our weapons, conducted more live-fire exercises, learned how to drive the heavier up-armored Humvees, and got our first training on the specialized communications equipment aboard each vehicle. In part because of all the new equipment, the few days before we went into Iraq were an exceptionally critical and busy time. After we recertified the training from Camp Shelby, we began a last two weeks of on-the-job mentorship.

The unit we replaced at Camp Navistar, the 1-178th Field Artillery from the South Carolina National Guard, provided the best training we received: hands-on, on-the-road, learning the job from the soldiers who had performed it for the entire preceding year.

After two weeks working with 1-178th, our Transfer of Authority ceremony on September 1 signified our assumption of the mission. During this ceremony our battle streamers and those of the 1-178th were called out to honor past sacrifices and conflicts. Some good-natured north-south jibing flared up when we compared battle streamers and realized that our two battalions had fought each other at Chancellorsville, Gettysburg, and other Civil War battlefields. We'd also fought alongside each other in WWI and WWII. Now, a testament to democracy, we'd come together to support Iraq's fledging government.

Joseph Streeter

Joseph Streeter

LEFT:
Up-armored Humvees at Udairi Range in Kuwait. Our unit did not train with this type of Humvee prior to arriving in Kuwait except for a few brief familiarization and licensing exercises.

ABOVE:
A lone Humvee patrols a road on the outskirts of Camp Shelby.

The 2-127th's campaign streamers include:

- Bull Run
- Second Manassas
- Antietam
- Petersburg
- Cold Harbor
- Spotsylvania
- Atlanta
- Wilderness
- Chattanooga
- Gettysburg

- Chickamauga
- Murfreesborough
- Chancellorsville
- Fredricksburg
- Puerto Rico
- Meuse-Argonne
- Aisne-Marne
- Champaign-1918
- Alsace-1918
- Oise-Aisne

- Papua New Guinea X 2
- New Guinea
- Leyte
- Luzon

The 2-127th Infantry also deployed and staged at Fort Lewis, Washington, for the Berlin Crisis. But fortunately they were never sent overseas for that event.

Our unit awards include:

- French Croix de Guerre, Oise-Aisne
- Presidential Unit Citation, Papua
- HQ Company, additional Presidential Unit Citation, Leyte
- Company A, Meritorious Unit Citation, New Guinea
- Meritorious Unit Citation, Operation Iraqi Freedom

Training didn't stop just because we'd begun our mission. Throughout the year new equipment arrived and soldiers learned to use it. In its constant efforts to improve safety during our missions, in spring 2006 our higher headquarters, 3rd Army, introduced a training device that mounted the chassis of a Humvee on a fulcrum and replicated the action of a vehicle in an accident or rollover, allowing our crews to practice pulling the gunner to safety in the cabin and then extracting themselves while upside-down. Refresher training, especially on marksmanship and medical skills, was also critical throughout our deployment.

Our particular mission, traveling all the roads in Iraq, made us ideal candidates for rapidly fielding new and experimental equipment. One soldier unofficially counted more than twenty-five additions and improvements to our Humvees during the year, everything from improved armor and bumpers to fire blankets and seat belts. We put a lot of miles and use on our gear, and our teams cycled back to home base at Navistar regularly enough to get debriefed on what worked and what didn't work on the last mission and to receive new training and equipment for the next. This process kept the soldiers from getting into a rut—and was the cause of more than a little grumbling as the teams had to clean out their trucks 100 percent before sending them to maintenance for the latest improvement.

But it gradually made our jobs safer.

The entire military experience, from basic training until your boots cross the border into a war zone, is nothing but training. It all adds up, every experience, into preparation for that moment when you undertake to perform a live mission, with live bullets, in a land where law and order are not the norm. At that moment, looking side to side, you see your buddies, the guys with whom you've trained, laughed, and struggled. And at that moment you realize that the process of becoming a professional soldier boils down to one thing: bonding. You cross the border, face the bullet, not because you've been trained to do it but because the last thing you'd ever do is let the guy beside you down.

Sergeant First Class Todd Peterson operates a device that simulates a Humvee rollover.

Joseph Streeter

Nathan Olson

LEFT:
Weapons require sights and optics to be zeroed in order to put rounds where the shooter intends them to go. Here, targets at Udairi Range are seen through the close-combat optic (CCO) mounted on an M4 carbine, the standard individual weapon carried by most of our soldiers.

ABOVE:
One of the least enjoyable but most realistic training events: sticking each other with IVs. You always tried to avoid the guy with shaky hands when selecting a partner for this training.

Photograph contributed by a member of the 2-127th

Joseph Streeter

Update Letter to Families
from Battalion Commander Lieutenant Colonel Todd Taves
June 16, 2005

Hello from Camp Shelby! The Battalion arrived safely on the ground one week ago today and has been busy ever since. Soldiers have completed initial readiness processing (dental, medical, finance, etc.), mandatory briefings, and are currently in an individual training program that will last a few more weeks before the units proceed to collective training at the platoon and company level. Current training is focused on tasks including first aid, weapons marksmanship, communications, and driver's training, among others. This training will ensure all soldiers are proficient at the basic skills needed to perform our mission overseas.

The weather, as expected, is very hot. The pace of our training is geared to allow soldiers the time to become accustomed to operating in the excessive heat. We have all learned very quickly that you must continuously drink water throughout the day to stay hydrated. Gatorade is a favorite and sells out quickly at the PX (base store).

After spending the first several days in a "Forward Operating Base" (FOB), soldiers are now living in a barracks area and have access to phones and the Internet and are receiving your mail and packages (fills a van every day!). The balance of our time here at Camp Shelby will be spent between the FOBs and the barracks area. While operating from the FOBs, phone and Internet access becomes more difficult, but Camp Shelby is working to improve this for us.

The 4th of July will be the first "day off" for the soldiers, and we will be organizing activities for them to participate in. I have received some questions as to whether family members can visit their soldiers on the 4th. We will allow for this; however, please be aware that soldiers will not be allowed to leave the post that day and will begin training again promptly the next morning.

Lastly, on behalf of the soldiers of the Gator Battalion, I would like to thank all those who participated in the various community sendoffs as well as the Battalion sendoff at Volk

Field. The support we have received has been absolutely tremendous, and we appreciate it. I will continue to post updates to this site periodically as we move through different phases of our training and deployment. From all of us here, we hope this message finds you well as we keep you in our thoughts.

Update Letter to Families
from Battalion Commander Lieutenant Colonel Todd Taves
July 5, 2005

Coming off our 4th of July holiday, the Gator Battalion is nearing the "halfway" mark of our training here at Camp Shelby. Training to this point has focused on individual soldiers' skills, and in the weeks ahead will shift to operating at the squad and platoon level with an emphasis on the tasks that we will perform as part of our overseas mission. At the end of this week, soldiers will also be moving back out into the Forward Operating Base (FOB) and spending several nights sleeping in the field.

Our soldiers have received many favorable comments from the trainers here and are doing an outstanding job that you can all be proud of. We are also becoming accustomed to training in the heat and humidity, and many soldiers have begun to notice their pants fitting a bit looser!

At the end of last month, I and several other leaders from the Battalion had the opportunity to travel to Kuwait and Iraq to see first hand where our soldiers will be based, and to observe the types of missions they will perform. Your soldiers were given an extensive briefing last week on what to expect. I can tell you that the living conditions will be quite good. The food is plentiful and good, there is air conditioned sleeping quarters, and a wide range of recreational opportunities such as movies, a gym, a recreation tent with Internet access and several food vendors such as Subway, Pizza Hut, and Green Beans Coffee, with most facilities open 24 hours per day.

OPPOSITE:
At Kuwait's Udairi Range in April, crews refreshed their marksmanship skills. The weather in the winter was actually quite cold, with a lot of rain and cloud cover so that good portions of the desert turned green as grass sprung up on every dune. The grass was short-lived, however, and by the time April rolled around, temperatures soared back into the 90s and 100s.

The soldiers that we will be replacing are also National Guardsmen, and we spent an extensive amount of time with them planning and preparing to take over their mission. I am confident that we have been given a mission that the Gator Battalion will be able to perform well, and that will challenge our soldiers on a daily basis.

The Battalion's graduation ceremony from training is currently scheduled for Wednesday, August 10. In about a week we will have a firmer plan as to when the Battalion will actually depart overseas, and how much time soldiers may be allowed off prior to that departure date. This information will be disseminated through the Battalion's Rear Detachment Commander Captain Kevin Agen as soon as we are able to confirm details. Thank you for your continued support.

Joseph Streeter

CHAPTER 2

Our Mission

During our year-long deployment, the 2-127th completed 5,232 combat missions, traveling more than 5,700,000 miles in a single year. The nature of our mission, convoy escort, made travel through the most dangerous regions of Iraq unavoidable. Our soldiers faced hostile action daily as a matter of course.

During this time our troops came into contact with the enemy 321 times, including 138 attacks by improvised explosive devices (IEDs), 124 small arms attacks (automatic rifle fire), eight attacks by indirect fire, seven complex attacks (combination of IED, small arms, and/or mortars), and forty-four attempts to steal trucks from convoys.

Joseph Streeter

Two convoys pass each other south of An-Nasiriyah.

Joseph Streeter

Joseph Streeter

ABOVE LEFT:

Two convoys pass each other on Main Supply Route (MSR) Tampa, one heading north toward Baghdad, the other returning to Camp Navistar after a long mission.

ABOVE RIGHT:

Crossing Sapper Bridge, near Baquba.

BELOW:

A convoy turns off the main supply route into CSC Cedar II.

Five tasks formed the core of our mission:

1. The escort and security of theater-wide troop and supply movements.
2. The escort and security of local sustainment convoys (carrying water, food, basic supplies).
3. Route security for the first 40 kilometers of the main supply route north to Baghdad.
4. The escort and security of vehicle recovery operations (wreckers) for the first 40 kilometers of the main supply route.
5. Special escort missions (escorting VIPs and local liaison missions).

Joseph Streeter

Joseph Streeter

ABOVE LEFT:
Sergeant Jeffrey Diederichs waits while his Humvee is refueled.

ABOVE RIGHT:
One of Saddam's many palaces, this one in Baghdad within the perimeter of BIAP (the military complex surrounding Baghdad International Airport).

LEFT:
Anytime a convoy stopped, even in the most inhospitable desert, Iraqis approached us, usually to try to sell things.

Joseph Streeter

Joseph Streeter

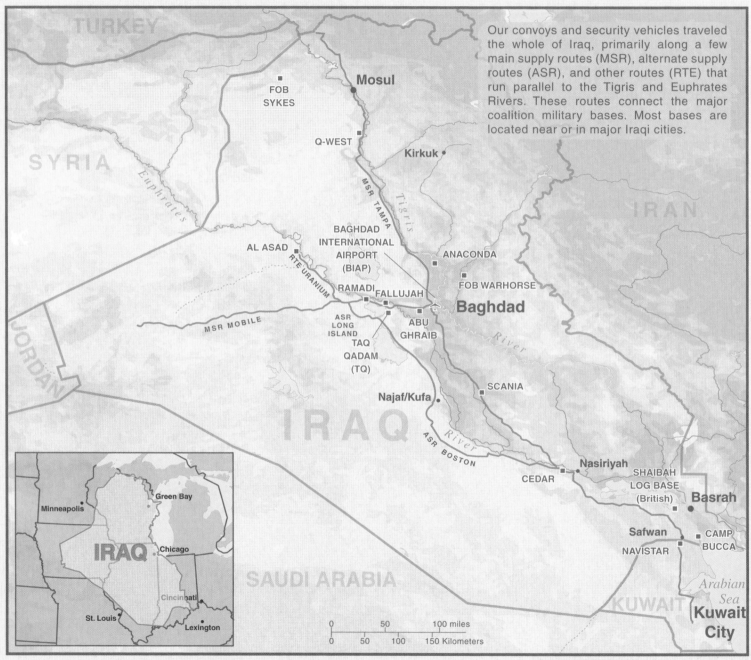

Our convoys and security vehicles traveled the whole of Iraq, primarily along a few main supply routes (MSR), alternate supply routes (ASR), and other routes (RTE) that run parallel to the Tigris and Euphrates Rivers. These routes connect the major coalition military bases. Most bases are located near or in major Iraqi cities.

TURKEY

SYRIA

Mosul

FOB SYKES

Q-WEST

Kirkuk

IRAN

MSR TAMPA

Tigris

Euphrates

BAGHDAD INTERNATIONAL AIRPORT (BIAP)

AL ASAD

ANACONDA

FOB WARHORSE

RTE URANIUM

RAMADI

FALLUJAH

Baghdad

MSR MOBILE

ABU GHRAIB

ASR LONG ISLAND

TAQ QADAM (TQ)

River

JORDAN

SCANIA

IRAQ

Najaf/Kufa

ASR BOSTON

River

Nasiriyah

SHAIBAH LOG BASE (British)

Basrah

CEDAR

Green Bay

Minneapolis

Chicago

IRAQ

Safwan

NAVISTAR

CAMP BUCCA

Cincinnati

SAUDI ARABIA

Arabian Sea

St. Louis

Lexington

KUWAIT

Kuwait City

0   50   100 miles
0 50 100   150 Kilometers

UW–Madison, Dept. of Geography, Cartography Lab

We provided security for all major deployment and redeployment ground movements conducted for Operation Iraqi Freedom from August 2005 to August 2006, including the 1st Armored Division, 1st Infantry Division, 1st Cavalry Division, 3rd Infantry Division, 4th Infantry Division, 35th Infantry Division, 42nd Infantry Division, 82nd Airborne Division, 101st Airborne Division, 1st Marine Expeditionary Force, 3rd Armored Cavalry Regiment, 11th Armored Cavalry Regiment, 172nd Stryker Brigade, 1-34th Brigade Combat Team, 48th Brigade Combat Team, 56th Brigade Combat Team, 116th Brigade Combat Team, and 3rd COSCOM (Corps Support Command).

Our security vehicles traveled to forty-three coalition bases and facilities all over Iraq:

the Green Zone

Fallujah

Taji

FOB (Forward Operating Base) Delta

FOB Dogwood

FOB Kalsu

FOB Charlie

FOB Warhorse

FOB Caldwell

FOB Falcon

FOB Rustimayah

FOB Loyalty

Abu Ghraib

Balad/LSA Anaconda

FOB Honor

Camp Bucca

Northport (Umm Qasr)

Southport (Umm Qasr)

Basrah

Shaibah Log Base

Tallil Air Base

CSC (Convoy Support Center) Cedar II

FOB Smitty

FOB Echo

FOB Duke

CSC Scania

BIAP (Baghdad International Airport)

FOB Brassfield-Mora

FOB Speicher

FOB Summerall

Remagen

Taq Qadum (TQ)

Ramadi

FOB Hit

FOB Corregidor

Al Asad Air Base

FOB Warrior

FOB Marez

FOB Diamondback

Q-West

FOB Sykes

FOB Iskandariyah

Nathan Olson

Responsibilities on Convoy Duty

On most missions three security vehicles, up-armored Humvees, accompanied a combination of thirty or more civilian and military semis. The convoys traveled with minimal supervision. Decisions made by young drivers, gunners, and vehicle commanders determined not only the success of the mission but also the safety of the crews and vehicles.

Each vehicle had a crew of three, with the capacity to carry two additional passengers (although they rarely did). Each crew member had a specific function. The driver, obviously, drove—but driving in combat is different from civilian driving, of course. The driver was responsible for keeping civilian vehicles at the proper distance, for avoiding potholes and debris in the road (which could damage the vehicle or even conceal improvised explosive devices, or IEDs), and for scanning a portion of the road, usually to his front and left. The gunner stood in the turret or sat on a strap at the "nametag defilade" position (keeping himself covered at least to the nametag on his uniform), which allowed him to see out of the turret but be best protected. His responsibility was to scan forward, backward, and to the side in the moving turret. He also used hand and arm signals to keep the semis in order and to warn away Iraqi civilian vehicles when necessary. Sitting in the passenger seat, the vehicle commander controlled all the activity in the Humvee. He was the senior-ranking person in the vehicle, usually a sergeant but sometimes a specialist. He operated all the complex communication equipment, navigated the roads, directed the gunner to fire if necessary, and scanned a portion of the road himself.

One important thing we understood: Our vehicles shared the roads with local Iraqis and passed through cities and villages where life slowly has begun to take on a more natural rhythm after twenty-five years of almost constant war and embargo. Very few Iraqis were insurgents. It was easy to slip into a mindset that everything was hostile, but that idea proved counterproductive. We needed to be wary, but truly the vast majority of Iraqis used the highways peacefully as we moved among them.

It was the convoy commander's responsibility to choose the route for each mission based on where the cargo in the convoy was destined to be delivered. In the first few months our soldiers did a lot of extra footwork at each camp we stopped at, trying to find the most current route maps and sources of intelligence. Most often we followed one main road from Kuwait City to Baghdad and Mosul.

Before each mission, and each day as the convoy moved from base to base, our security personnel met with the convoy commander. Together they decided what tactics to employ. They discussed known danger areas. Often they became friends, with transportation commanders asking for particular security personnel by name on future missions.

One security Humvee usually led the convoy and another almost always brought up the rear, protecting each end. The third Humvee moved up and down the line, its crew watching for trouble.

OPPOSITE:
Before every mission, the convoy leader conducted a mission briefing to update the soldiers on threats along the way, weather, routes to the base, his plan for movement (which Humvee would take which place in the convoy), and other critical issues.

RIGHT:

Soldiers meet at the front of the trucks just before a night movement. They make sure everyone knows the route, go over the most current threats, and discuss the actions to take in the event of an attack.

Joseph Streeter

Joseph Streeter

ABOVE:

A child in a Green Bay Packers sweatshirt waves to our passing Humvees as we conduct a patrol around Safwan.

Keeping It Together

Our soldiers encountered many challenges on the road. One of the biggest was communication. With a hundred meters or more between each vehicle, the length of the convoy could stretch several kilometers.

Crews communicated internally with hands-free headset/microphone devices. Flipping a switch on the device enabled us to broadcast messages to other vehicles in the convoy over encrypted radio. The range of this radio usually extended only ten or fifteen kilometers. With convoys traveling the length and breadth of Iraq, a small dashboard-mounted computer enabled each vehicle to communicate with each other and with battalion headquarters by text messages sent via satellite. The troops on the road could report their position and any significant or suspicious events, and headquarters could send threat and weather updates.

Of the convoy's semis, only a few were military. The drivers of the civilian-contracted semis often spoke Urdu or Arabic or Hindi, turning the convoy into a rolling Tower of Babel. Communication between the contracted drivers and our soldiers required the presence of one hired interpreter on each convoy (some of whom knew only a smattering of English), or the creative use of gestures and pre-fabricated picture cards captioned in multiple languages.

Nathan Olson

Contracted convoy drivers lived with their vehicles, sleeping in them while on missions, eating in them or around them, playing soccer in the semi staging lots, even setting up their hookah pipes nearby and sitting in informal groups.

Joseph Streeter

ABOVE:

Pumping fuel into the Humvee was just one of many small but necessary tasks our soldiers completed in order to be successful in the larger mission.

ABOVE RIGHT:

Specialist Daniel Micoley checks the oil in his team's Humvee, one of the steps in the PMCS (preventive maintenance checks and services) performed on all equipment prior to a mission.

RIGHT:

Contracted drivers wait for the start of a mission.

Nathan Olson

Along with protecting convoys from enemy action, each guntruck crew performed many other tasks: inspecting vehicles prior to the beginning of each mission; navigating the roads to ensure the convoys did not make a wrong turn en route from base to base, exposing them to the risk of trying to turn thirty semis around in a tight place; performing communications checks with other units as the convoys passed from one region of Iraq to the next; reporting suspicious activity or critical events back to battalion headquarters; and maintaining the Humvee, its weapon systems, and its crew.

Joseph Streeter

Joseph Streeter

Sergeant Ken Zubich conducts an inspection as a contracted driver looks on.

Dangers on the Road

Some missions were one-day, round-trip journeys to the first base on the route north, which usually took about eight hours. Other missions, heading farther north, required multiple stops. Depending on the distance, these assignments lasted between five and fifteen days, with each leg of the journey taking three to eight hours—a long time on the road, no matter how you broke it up.

Vehicle crew members became very close friends, even if personalities clashed (though they rarely did). When things went wrong, those friendships were brought into sharper focus. We often encountered small arms fire—usually just a few tracer rounds from the side of the road, but some attacks lasted an hour or more while the convoy was stopped for other reasons. If our gunners identified the source of fire, they returned the favor.

Improvised explosive devices were the most common, and most dangerous, threat we encountered on the roads. Some of these devices were very complex, modern weapons imported by militant groups. Others were handmade collections of nuts and bolts wrapped around whatever explosive was available to the bomb-maker. They varied accordingly in their deadliness. IEDs usually targeted the lead vehicle in the convoy. Camouflaged on the shoulder of the road and triggered anonymously, these could be small and still wreak havoc. Another common danger was complex attacks, IEDs accompanied by small arms fire.

Indirect fire (anything lobbed from a position out of sight or behind an obstacle) was a rare occurrence on these missions, but while resting and refueling at the bases along the route, we experienced quite a few mortar attacks.

Hijackings, on the other hand, were not uncommon. At over $40,000 for the truck, plus the value of the cargo, these semis presented a sore temptation to Iraqis earning $350 a month. Some Iraqis specialized in stealing trucks from convoys.

Of course we also had our share of vehicle breakdowns and accidents. Tires blew out, trucks ran over debris in the road, engines overheated. Usually the entire convoy would wait, guarding the disabled vehicle, until a wrecker vehicle under armed escort and dispatched from the nearest base arrived. Likewise, injuries were almost unavoidable. Our soldiers were trained in advanced lifesaving skills and could call for medevac airlift when needed, and we used medevac transport more than twenty times over the course of our mission.

Joseph Streeter

A convoy rolls north through a sandstorm.

Nathan Olson

RIGHT:

One of several wrecker trucks based at Camp Navistar contracted to haul damaged semis and Humvees off the road to safety. Each base along the route north had these contracted crews, and each was responsible for a large amount of roadway.

BELOW RIGHT:

Staff Sergeant Tyler Gerrits and Sergeant Jeffrey Diederichs received the Soldier's Medal for valor—the Army's highest award for actions not in contact with the enemy. On October 14, 2005, Gerrits and Diederichs responded to a burning Humvee with several soldiers trapped inside. Heedless of the risk to themselves, as ammunition from inside the vehicle exploded in the fire and the soles of their own boots melted to the roof of the Humvee, Gerrits and Diederichs pulled one of the trapped men from the flames.

Joseph Streeter

Joseph Streeter

Joseph Streeter

Joseph Streeter

ABOVE:
The 1158th Transportation Company from Janesville, another Wisconsin National Guard unit, was in Iraq with us. We provided security for them on several occasions.

ABOVE:

Two soldiers, forged by training into a team, look across the desert on their first mission. That first mission would be a lonely experience if not for the bonds of camaraderie formed during training.

LEFT:

One of our soldiers mans a .50cal machine gun as his convoy stops on the side of the road. He also has a M240B machine gun as his secondary weapon system, in case of a malfunction with the .50. On most missions, our soldiers never shot. Encounters with the enemy were frequent but often amounted to a remotely detonated IED, allowing us no chance to return fire. Sometimes, though, as the convoys rolled through hot-spots, gunners would positively identify the source of shots fired at them. The vehicle commander would then authorize the gunner to return fire. As a gunner you never knew when it might happen, and when it did occur it happened so quickly that rarely did we know the results.

Joseph Streeter

Route Security Element

While the majority of our unit performed convoy escort throughout all of Iraq, a smaller group—about the size of a platoon, flexing between eight and sixteen vehicles—patrolled the first 40 miles of the main highway leading from Kuwait to Baghdad. This group, called the Route Security Element, or RSE, operated in teams of two vehicles.

The Route Security Element worked with a large degree of autonomy. Its responsibilities included clearing all debris from the road and the shoulders to reduce opportunities for insurgents to camouflage IEDs among the debris, keeping a presence in and around Safwan to deter criminals from hijacking trucks from our convoys, escorting convoys with damaged or malfunctioning vehicles to safety, conducting random checkpoints to search vehicles for contraband such as bomb-making equipment and unregistered weapons, and reporting on local conditions and "atmospherics"—a general sense of the feel of the community that day.

At first the RSE duties were rotated throughout the battalion. It soon became apparent, though, that these crews needed to develop a detailed understanding of the area in which they worked, an understanding best learned through experience. Lieutenant Colonel Taves assigned this task to a single platoon, led by First Lieutenant Eric Krueger, a police officer from Horicon, and Sergeant First Class John Dietzler, a correctional officer from Green Bay. Their law enforcement background contributed to the success of RSE's mission, largely a policing operation.

Our RSE links up with a British patrol before an operation. The RSE operated in a British area in Basra Province and focused on rebuilding efforts. Working in the same battle space as the British, we needed close coordination. We worked with the British through all levels of our battalion and fostered many close relationships, most notably the daily interaction between the RSE and British patrols.

Joseph Streeter

Joseph Streeter

Joseph Streeter

Two RSE patrol members question an Iraqi youth about unexploded ordnance found nearby.

Joseph Streeter

Seven hired interpreters assisted the RSE, riding along on all shifts. An Arabic translator was a necessity because few Iraqis spoke English well enough to interact with our teams; likewise, none of our soldiers spoke Arabic, although many picked up a few words through interaction with the Iraqis and the interpreters. These seven served us well, teaching us about Islamic culture and a little about the language—by the end of our mission, most RSE team members could conduct some basic questioning in Arabic. Equally important, in a number of situations our interpreters took the lead, not just advising us on the cultural aspect of a pending confrontation but using our troops' general guidance to resolve crises. For example, when one of our trucks hit an Iraqi house, our RSE team told the interpreter to "keep the people back" and "get hold of the police" while our troops worked on the situation. The interpreter organized local Iraqi men to help keep curious people at bay, called the police chief on his personal cell phone, and even tackled one young man who moved into the area to try to steal things. The interpreters also joined us at meetings in the town council to decipher delicate political meanings and technical terms about rebuilding and finances.

Benjamin Buchholz

Benjamin Buchholz

Joseph Streeter

ABOVE:

Our RSE interpreters, from left to right: Mohammed el-Sayel, Chadi Deabies, Adel "Snowman" Omar, Nadal Qasem, Bashar "Bob" al-Masri, and Wael "Willy" Mahmoud.

LEFT:

Willy speaks with a retired police officer without a pension, whose entire family income is generated by his son's store. (An interview with his son, Hussein Khazim, starts on page 92.)

ABOVE:

One of our interpreters, Sayer Thuwainy Sayer, aka Sam, obtained his Kuwaiti citizenship in March and could no longer go north of the border with us. Converting from Bedouin (with no official country) to Kuwaiti citizenship was a great benefit to Sam and his family, as they now shared in the Kuwaiti state's oil wealth. However, after the wars with Iraq Kuwaiti law prohibited Kuwaitis from entering Iraq. Sam did invite a few members from the RSE to a traditional celebration in a Bedouin camp. Here he demonstrates how to eat from the communal platter of lamb and rice.

RIGHT:

A little like a traffic stop in the United States, RSE sets up a flash vehicle checkpoint in the shade of a highway overpass. A flash checkpoint differs from a permanent checkpoint in that it is set up temporarily, on the go, in order to interdict a suspicious vehicle. Here the team motions a driver to pull over.

Joseph Streeter

Joseph Streeter

Joseph Streeter

ABOVE LEFT: As the first driver pulls over and hands his ID to the RSE team leader, a second car also stops, waiting in line to be checked. RSE motions this second car to continue when they decide to search the first vehicle in greater detail. The driver of the first vehicle appears nervous and fits the demographic for the young male Iraqi whom our teams have been taught to suspect, and he has a very old ID card, a sign that he may be trying to avoid official records. The second driver, waiting patiently in line even after RSE waved him through the checkpoint, appears calm and perfectly ready to go through the checkpoint.

ABOVE RIGHT: The passengers sit on the side of the road as the driver moves around the vehicle with the RSE team members. The RSE teams search by hand, looking through any part of the car that might contain weapons, explosives, or other contraband. These stops were random and quick.

Joseph Streeter

LEFT:
The interpreter, standing between Sergeant Chad Walker and Sergeant Adam Robinson, asks the driver to get out of the car and open all the doors, the hood, the trunk, the glove compartment, and even the gas tank.

LEFT:
In the end, as in most such random checks, the RSE team finds nothing. The driver and his passengers are allowed to continue on their way, with instructions to get a new ID card. Iraqis have become accustomed to such vehicle checkpoints, and most of those who aren't smuggling contraband or involved in illegal activities support them.

Joseph Streeter

RIGHT:

RSE cleans debris off the road, removing anything that could puncture a tire on a convoy vehicle. They more carefully remove larger items that could conceal improvised explosive devices. When the RSE did find an IED (or suspect an object to be an IED), they would cordon it off and put in a call through our battalion TOC to the British Explosive Ordnance Disposal (EOD) teams in the region. Due to the volume of unexploded ordnance and the number of IED incidents, the EOD teams were stretched thin. RSE often had to hold its cordon around a suspected object for several hours before it could be cleared.

FAR RIGHT:

Sergeant Robinson marks an old landmine with spray paint so an Explosive Ordnance Disposal (EOD) team can remove it.

Joseph Streeter

The RSE's work in Iraq is a deterrent to criminal and insurgent activity. The 2-127th's RSE presence around Safwan was the only U.S. presence in an area otherwise overseen by British troops. Thus our soldiers were representatives of everything "American" to these Iraqis. Through interpreters, meetings with town officials, and patrolling along the main road in town the RSE conducted an operation that not only kept the roads safer but also contributed to the stabilization of Safwan, allowing fledging democratic institutions to take root.

Joseph Streeter

Update Letter to Families
from Battalion Commander Lieutenant Colonel Todd Taves
August 22, 2005

I am happy to report that the soldiers of the 2-127 have all arrived safely in Kuwait as of August 20th. The Battalion is presently occupying two different camps: Camp Navistar, where we will be stationed permanently, and Camp Buehring, where some of our soldiers will be staying temporarily for the next three weeks. For now, there is not enough room for everyone to stay at Navistar until the Battalion we are replacing begins its movement back to the United States.

Facilities at both locations include air conditioned sleeping areas, a gymnasium, a Post Exchange, fast food restaurants, and other small stores and recreation facilities. You will probably hear from your soldiers that the food is great! The dining facility serves four meals per day (including a midnight meal for those soldiers that work the night shift).

As expected, the weather is extremely hot and dry with temperatures peaking into 115°+ range daily. The good news is that August is the hottest month of the year, and we can expect to see daytime temperatures begin to drop in the next few weeks. While the heat does impact our operations, our time spent in the hot Camp Shelby environment was good preparation and most soldiers are holding up great.

During the next three weeks, your soldiers will be undertaking the final preparations for their mission. This includes signing for their armored Humvees, conducting additional weapons range firing, and participating on missions with the soliders that we are replacing. This allows us to benefit from the experience of the soldiers that have been performing our mission for the past year.

We will continue to keep you updated on our progress as our mission proceeds. Thank you for your continued support.

Benjamin Buchholz

ABOVE:
This flag, probably sent in a care package, had no ceremonies or parades to wave at, but it found a home here on Becker's bedpost.

RIGHT:
Specialist Etzel and tentmate Specialist Adam Malwitz share a true tent luxury, one of the few couches in camp.

INTERVIEW
Specialist Thomas Etzel
and Sergeant Nathan Becker

For many of the younger troops (and perhaps a few of the older ones) this deployment repre-sented a first time away from home—new cul-ture, new land, new duties and values as a full-time soldier. Many of our young men weren't shocked by these changes, but they matured in little ways, while keeping their devilish high spirits.

Specialist Etzel and Sergeant Becker repre-sent the vast majority of those who answered the call to arms: young, with the best part of their lives ahead of them, well-educated, articu-late, and ready to apply themselves to the task at hand.

Specialist Thomas Etzel, from Campbells-port, is twenty-two. He's going to college at UW–Stevens Point for web and digital media design. He's got a new girlfriend back home,

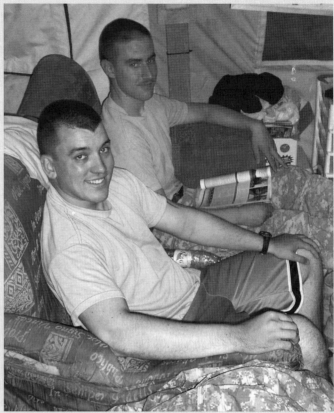

Benjamin Buchholz

introduced to him online by one of the guys in his squad. They met over mid-tour leave and have been dating by email ever since.

Sergeant Nathan Becker, promoted from the rank of specialist while deployed, recently graduated from Carthage College in Kenosha. He married his college sweetheart, Nikki, just before mobilization. He hails from Beaver Dam.

What do you miss most about home?

SPC Etzel: Being able to drive my own car. I miss my dad's chili, going up to Crivitz out in the country and on the boat. Going to car shows.

SGT Becker: Being able to drive a car—the Humvee feels like driving an ice chest. I miss going to Brewers and Badger games. I have Badger football season tickets, just got them last year, and I haven't even had a chance to use them, missed Barry Alvarez's last year.

How has your perception of home changed since coming here?

SPC Etzel: I realize I've taken a lot of little things for granted: fresh bread, showering at a temperature I like (not *just* hot water). Being able to go to any of a number of stores and get little stuff I want. Sleeping in. Hanging out with friends. Soft beds. I've noticed on leave that a

Benjamin Buchholz

LEFT:
Sergeant Becker's "Happy Wall," featuring a picture of his wife, Nikki, along with a keepsake photo of two hippie musicians he met at a campsite in the Northwoods.

BELOW LEFT:
Specialist Etzel helps Private First Class Jeremy Fritz with his "crappy mustache."

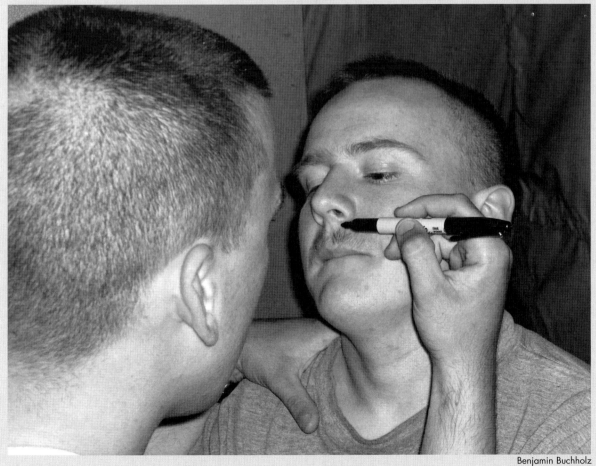

Benjamin Buchholz

47

Benjamin Buchholz

ABOVE:

Some of the strange items found in Specialist Etzel's bunk area: wicked clowns?

RIGHT:

Sergeant (then Specialist) Becker enjoys some tea brought out to him by an Iraqi while on patrol with the Route Security Element.

Photo contributed by a member of the 2-127th

lot of people complain back home about miniscule unimportant things like how hot it is outside, food temperatures at restaurants, rudeness at a store, always needing a better car. Those things are so unimportant.

SGT Becker: It seemed surreal being home on leave. I found myself thinking, "Are you kidding me? I'm actually back." It seems so far away now, in both time and place. I don't know what I'd do without phones and email here. The guys in Desert Storm didn't have that stuff. I can't imagine.

How do you like living communally in the tents? Any funny stories?

SPC Etzel: It depends. There are good days and bad days. All in all it hasn't been that bad.

One time we got care packages with maxi-pads in them (we're an infantry unit with all guys, so not much use for them). We took the backings off and taped them all over our buddy's area. Another time we all grew crappy mustaches and took a photo shoot of ourselves. We play pranks on each other, told PFC Fritz that the command sergeant major wanted to see him. He got all dressed up in his best uniform, shaved, showered, nervous, and then just before he went in to the CSM's room we told him it was a prank.

SGT Becker: As for the tents, we're crowded in this one—eight guys is too much, I think. It's not like college where you have a home with five roommates and some elbow room or a place you can be alone.... In any group of eight dudes someone is bound to smell bad. We've got mice too. Seven of them caught in the last month. Mattice and Wilhelms in my tent have the nastiest bunk areas because they never lived away from their moms, and mom would just clean up for them. So, big shock for them living without a maid.

Do any of your tentmates have weird habits?

SGT Becker: One time Mattice ran around in a thong his girlfriend sent him. It was pouring rain. He went swimming in just this little white thong and then someone turned on music and he was dancing around a pole. Funny but weird. Also, Staff Sergeant Walker used to mess with people's stuff. It got annoying after a while, so when he went on leave we took all the sandbags we could find and filled his whole area with them—three hundred or so. It took him about four hours to clean it out when he got back. He was pissed, but he laughs about it now.

Benjamin Buchholz

ABOVE:
A visual comment on faith: Luther and the iPod.

LEFT:
Sergeant Becker and others conspired to leave a surprise for their squad leader when he returned from mid-tour leave—a bunk full of sandbags.

Photo contributed by a member of the 2-127th

49

RIGHT:

Specialist Schussler in football gear, laughing with a teammate. Schussler plays defense for St. Norbert College. He maintained his workout routine while deployed and was able to rejoin the team in time for the 2006 season.

Benjamin Buchholz

ABOVE:

Seth Schussler kept this article on his younger brother Tharin taped to his tent wall. The article talks about Seth and Tyler at war.

RIGHT:

Seth's photos from home include one of his girlfriend, Ashley.

INTERVIEW
Specialist Seth Schussler

Soldiers come from all walks of life and in all shapes and sizes. Several members of the 2-127th, over here doing hands-on work as team leaders, are lawyers or business executives back home. Others are electricians, prison guards, truck drivers, schoolteachers. Unlike active duty soldiers who specialize in their trade, National Guard soldiers bring an additional wealth of civilian experience with them.

Specialist Seth Schussler has one of the most interesting careers of our soldiers. An imposing figure at about 6'4", 280 pounds, he plays college football for St. Norbert College in Green Bay. He forfeited his sophomore season to join up with our unit and completed basic training just two months prior to our deployment.

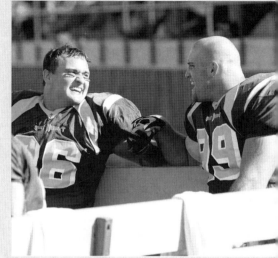

Photograph courtesy of the St. Norbert College football program

One of Schussler's three brothers, Tyler, also deployed with us. The Schusslers are one of several sets of brothers or father-and-son combinations in the 2-127th. Others include the Jaworski brothers; First Sergeant Fritz and his son, Jeremy Fritz; and Andrew Neumeyer and his brother Eric, who was sent home on compassionate leave after Andrew was seriously wounded. Specialist Dylan Posselt, unable to deploy with us because he had not yet completed basic training, had his father call us after his first drill weekend. Usually that's a bad sign. But his dad said, "Hey, this sounds like fun. Can I sign up?" He finished basic training before his son and fought in Iraq as a member of our battalion.

I know you've got a serious girlfriend back home. Any secrets for how you've managed to stay together?

SPC Schussler: We've been dating for two years now, but we were only together for six months before I came over here. I've been talking to a lot of guys who have been having troubles with their relationships, but it seems like Ashley and I are doing okay. A big thing for us is that she has stayed really close to my family. She babysits my youngest brother, Riley, who is twelve, and her little brother is the same age, so they like hanging out together.

Benjamin Buchholz

What do you miss about home?

SPC Schussler: A big bed. My feet hang off my bed here. I miss having the room to roll around, but I've gotten used to it here, I guess.

How has your perception of home changed since coming here?

SPC Schussler: Being here has opened my eyes to how nice it is to be from small town America.

Benjamin Buchholz

I always thought it was nice, but before I left I thought it would be cool to go off and live someplace else. Now I realize I just want to live in my hometown. That'll be good enough for me.

How do you like living communally in the tents?

SPC Schussler: There are eight guys in my tent, and I'm the lowest-ranking one. So I've got about 3 square feet of living area. I barely fit in it. I like it though, the idea of living together. I like it more now than I did when we first got here because these guys are now my friends. You've always got someone to talk to, hang out with. When I look back on this war that will probably be one of my favorite parts. It's something a lot of people think about when they join up with the Army, that camaraderie. I'm happy to have found it. I've had a positive experience and learned it's all about your attitude. From football, I was used to a pretty structured existence. I think some guys have a hard time in this environment because it's the first time they've had a lot of rules to obey and a lot of people looking over their shoulder.

Any funny stories?

SPC Schussler: Specialist Krajenka and I have started to lift together. KJ usually sleeps like twenty-four hours a day when he can, but lately he's wanted to get built better. KJ will use a 3-pound weight when I do 55 or 75 pounds. But it's making the effort. And it's great to hang out together.

Photo contributed by a member of the 2-127th

ABOVE LEFT:
Nametags, sunglasses, and CDs strewn about the one bit of makeshift cabinet Schussler "owned."

ABOVE:
Schussler and KJ flex their "guns."

CHAPTER 3

Command Teams

Joseph Streeter

OPPOSITE:
First Sergeant Steven Fritz, B Company, talks to his troops.

LEFT:
Major Thomas O'Brien
Executive Officer
Hometown: Stevens Point

Lieutenant Colonel Todd Taves
Commander
Hometown: Waukesha

Command Sergeant Major Rafael Conde
Hometown: River Falls

Command of soldiers in war is the ultimate honor in our profession of arms. Everything the unit does or fails to do is the commander's legal and moral responsibility, and units often assume the character of their leaders. The ability to convince soldiers to do something despite known peril is the essence of military leadership. Military leaders make decisions that often put the lives of their troops at risk in order to accomplish the mission. That risk makes soldiering a unique profession.

2-127th Battalion Command Teams

INTERVIEW WITH LIEUTENANT COLONEL TODD TAVES

Did your perception of "war" change during this deployment?

LTC Taves: I think one way in which my perception of war may have changed would be as it relates to the idea of the "enemy." Having enlisted during the Cold War, it had always been my expectation that combat would involve massed formations of soldiers and armored vehicles, more similar to the first Gulf War. We certainly knew ahead of time that we were facing an insurgency with few visible targets, but having experienced it, it gives you an even better appreciation for the challenges of what the Army refers to as asymmetrical warfare. Most of the time when you are moving about in Iraq, you don't necessarily feel particularly threatened; however, danger is ever present, and a calm situation and environment can quickly turn deadly. The lack of an easily defined enemy is frustrating. Being "passersby" in our role as convoy escorts, it is nearly impossible to maintain the initiative, [which leaves] the insurgents with the ability to attack you at the time and place of their choosing. This was the reality that our soldiers had to deal with on a daily basis out on the road.

Joseph Streeter

Command Sergeant Major Conde and Lieutenant Colonel Taves

What one lesson from this deployment will stay with you?

LTC Taves: Without question, the amazing job that our young leaders did. Operating hundreds and sometimes thousands of miles from our operating base, we routinely had sergeants and staff sergeants executing missions and making decisions that would normally be made by lieutenants or higher. They did a commendable job and their efforts led directly to mission success. Our corps of non-commissioned officers experienced tremendous growth during the deployment.

If you could go back to just before deployment and change something, what would it be?

LTC Taves: In almost all respects, we were fortunate to be very well prepared for the deployment, and I can't really identify one particular thing that if changed would have had a material affect on the unit. We had a pretty frenzied sixty days of preparation at the mobilization station prior to departure for Kuwait. While we left fully prepared, I would have liked to have had another ten to fifteen days so that we could have spent a little more time on a few tasks and could have also given the unit a few more days of leave prior to departing. All in all, however, I thought the entire mobilization process went remarkably well, and I would change little.

There were a lot of pranks among your command team and staff. Any of them publishable?

LTC Taves: I think in the interests of decorum, specifics would not be appropriate. I think, however, that [the pranks show] the high level of esprit de corps and camaraderie of the personnel in the unit. Laughter is needed, even in a combat zone!

INTERVIEW WITH COMMAND SERGEANT MAJOR RAFAEL CONDE

What was your role as the command sergeant major here?

CSM Conde: The role of the CSM in our type of operation was different than I expected. I saw my role as one of making sure that all of our equipment and our soldiers were as ready as possible for the mission. This included looking into ways of making the guntrucks safer and enhancing their performance.

My role as the CSM was also to maintain discipline of the soldiers, while understanding that they needed space to relax and unwind after a mission. One reason that I did not conduct inspections of the tents was to allow the soldiers their own personal space. While I was adamant about fire safety, I was lenient on how the soldiers lived.

I made it a point to spend as much time as I could on the road—not just to get away from Arifjan, but to make sure that our soldiers were doing the right things on the road. The right things included wearing their PPE [personal protective equipment] and traveling in a protective posture. I was really proud of the job that the NCOs [non-commissioned officers] did in enforcing the standards while on the road. That is a sign of a disciplined unit.

"Be, Know, Do" is the motto of the NCO—which is most important?

CSM Conde: I believe that a soldier cannot be a great soldier without being all three. It is not enough to be a soldier, it is not enough to be the most tactically proficient soldier in the Army. It is enough to be a soldier who is tactically and technically proficient and to DO the things that make us a great Army.

So to answer the question, as Nike would say: Just DO it!

How important was physical fitness to our mission?

CSM Conde: Deployed soldiers in Operation Iraqi Freedom can attest to the grueling grind on the human body. With temperatures that could reach 150 degrees Fahrenheit inside the M1114 Humvee, even with a working air conditioner, physical fitness became immensely important for the success of the mission in Iraq. Soldiers also had to endure increased weight on their bodies due to protective gear. With ammo, body armor, and other items, the uniform could weigh 50 to 60 pounds.

Beyond the physical advantages of maintaining your body at a high level of physical fitness, it is a well-known fact that soldiers benefit emotionally from being physically fit. They feel better about themselves and reduce stress levels while engaged in physical activities.

One of your jobs was to be the enforcer of rules. We all know there are some rules that are just stupid. Where did you draw the line in choosing what to emphasize?

CSM Conde: The Army is full of rules and regulations; most of them exist to enhance discipline and to make sure that the entire organization is on the same sheet of music. Yet some regulations are provided for the safety of soldiers.

As the senior non-commissioned soldier in the battalion, I must enforce all regulations and policies as defined by the Army. Whether I believe they are correct or not is not relevant. We can, and should, try to change regulations that are not in the best interests of our soldiers, but until that change happens, we must comply with the rules.

The standards that I chose to overlook were the ones that did not make sense and were not in the best interest of the soldiers. One such policy was the wearing of the black fleece cap in Kuwait. When the standard came out that soldiers were not allowed to wear the knit cap in Kuwait even when the temperature was dipping into the mid 30s, I made a conscientious decision not to have my soldiers adhere to that standard. I was willing to alienate other CSMs for the protection of the men.

Alpha Company "Wolves"

Our battalion did not have enough soldiers to field four full companies, so the E Troop of the 105th Cavalry from Merrill and Antigo and the 32nd Engineer Company from Onalaska combined to carry the Alpha Company flag on this deployment. The original 2-127th Alpha Company soldiers were dispersed throughout the battalion.

INTERVIEW WITH CAPTAIN DALE ELLENBECKER

What was the toughest moment for you on this deployment?

CPT Ellenbecker: Casualties in general. All of them. I was standing there in the Tactical Operations Center watching the info come in on MTS [a military instant-messaging system] when I found out about Sergeant Jopek. I remember the words on the screen appearing, "KIA," and my heart just stopped. [When Specialist Neumeyer was injured] I went up to LSA Anaconda [a northern base] with his brother and we sat with Andrew in the hospital. Really tough to see one of your soldiers so injured, knowing he'd most likely be blind.

What was the best moment?

CPT Ellenbecker: I was pretty happy yesterday, because I found out I was headed home on the first airplane *and* I reached my twenty years of service, a big milestone. When Roland, Macias, and Stelzer got hit by the IED but despite serious injuries were still alive—that was another moment, a sigh of relief.

What have you learned from your troops?

CPT Ellenbecker: Nothing too profound but a lot of little things. Computer skills. I didn't know what a memory stick was until we got here. I learned that [these men] adapt well to adversity and that no matter how bad things got, they had the grit to continue the mission.

If, say, your own eighteen-year-old son or daughter wanted to join the military, what would you tell him or her?

First Sergeant
Richard Clay
Hometown: Antigo

Master Sergeant
Daniel Hong
Operations NCO
Hometown: Onalaska

First Lieutenant
Matthew Elder
Executive Officer
Hometown: Muscoda

Captain Dale Ellenbecker
Company Commander
Hometown: Mosinee

Nathan Olson

CPT Ellenbecker: I'd tell him it will make him a more well-rounded person for the rest of his life. In high school I couldn't have cared less about politics; now I follow them. I've learned what my personal weaknesses and strengths are. And no place teaches leadership better than the U.S. military.

INTERVIEW WITH FIRST SERGEANT RICHARD CLAY

This was a mission in which the young leaders, the sergeants and staff sergeants, had most of the responsibility out there on the road. What does that mean to you?

1SG Clay: This mission was the first time our sergeants and staff sergeants had to carry the whole responsibility on their shoulders. Back home they always had supervision, the platoon sergeants and platoon leaders. During this mission they didn't have that. It was a good experience for the future leadership of the National Guard.

What one skill, more than any other, makes a leader excellent?

1SG Clay: Taking care of and managing people. By "taking care of people," I mean the variety of [soldiers'] needs, and doing it for a longer time here than just the two weeks of an annual training back home. You saw a range of things here over a year, problems and issues, that most National Guard guys never see.

How important is military bearing?

1SG Clay: Somebody's always looking, always watching, so you've got to set the example. Just when you think you can get away with something, that's when the young soldier sees it and thinks it's okay.

As the most senior and experienced soldier in your company, how has your career prepared you for this deployment?

1SG Clay: Nothing really prepared me for this, though I've had a long, long career. Taking on a mixture of different companies when 32nd Engineers and the Cav merged—[it's] tough to forge bonds. It was overwhelming right away, but I'd try one thing, and if it worked, fine; if it didn't I'd try something else.

Bravo Company "Blacksheep"

INTERVIEW WITH CAPTAIN BRION ADERMAN

What was the toughest moment for you on this deployment?

CPT Aderman: September 26, when Sergeant Wallace and Specialist Wendling were lost. It was so early in the deployment, and [it] drove home how dangerous it was. It left us staring down the barrel at another eleven months. But it also helped us focus. I was Wallace's and Wendling's platoon leader prior to becoming Bravo Company commander, so I knew them well.

What was the best moment?

CPT Aderman: Plural, moments. Every mission I went on with my guys. I never went with the same crew twice, so I got to see a lot of them in action. It was great spending those days on the road getting to know the guys.

Nathan Olson

Captain Brion Aderman
Company Commander
Hometown: Milwaukee

First Lieutenant
Dean Nemecek
Executive Officer
Hometown: Green Bay

What have you learned from your troops?

CPT Aderman: No so much learned but [had] reinforced: Stay focused on taking care of soldiers. Everything else we tend to worry about is inconsequential. I was fortunate to work with a group of people who kept that in mind, my staff, my NCOs [non-commissioned officers].

If, say, your own eighteen-year-old son or daughter wanted to join the military, what would you tell him or her?

CPT Aderman: It's not an easy or comfortable or glamorous lifestyle, but like anything else worthwhile, the difficulties and work required tend to yield their own rewards. On a deployment like this you can choose to learn and grow, to take the challenges and persevere, become a better person for having dealt with them. Or you can choose to be bitter and to resist. I don't know what I would look like had I not joined the military when I was eighteen. It's a big part of me.

**First Sergeant
Steven Fritz
Hometown: Oshkosh**

INTERVIEW WITH FIRST SERGEANT STEVEN FRITZ

This was a mission where the young leaders, the sergeants and staff sergeants, had most of the responsibility out there on the road. What does that mean to you?

1SG Fritz: That's the level of leadership where the rubber meets the road in any operation—down in the trenches. The guys who have responsibility for the mission. Ultimately the success we've had rests squarely on them.

What one skill, more than any other, makes a leader excellent?

1SG Fritz: There's a saying I heard a while ago and keep repeating to people: "Soldiers don't care how much you know until they know how much you care." That's the heart of it.

How important is military bearing?

1SG Fritz: It's what separates a soldier from a civilian. It's the professional packet, the whole soldier: discipline, courtesy, integrity, Army values. What you see in a professional soldier should be what you get.

As the most senior and experienced soldier in your company, how has your career prepared you for this deployment?

1SG Fritz: Every year has been a stepping stone. If you apply yourself and become more and more professional as a soldier, hopefully it all comes together.

Charlie Company "Crusaders"

INTERVIEW WITH CAPTAIN ERIC SCHACK

What was the toughest moment for you on this deployment?

CPT Schack: The deaths of Sergeant Wallace and Specialist Wendling. I coped with the situation by thinking about what my soldiers wanted and deserved to see from me as their leader—the human aspect of it, the sadness, sharing that with them, but also the leadership aspect, continuing the mission despite the adversity.

What was the best moment?

CPT Schack: Every awards ceremony I was able to conduct was a best moment. The opportunity to recognize and reward my soldiers for what they did on the battlefield.

What have you learned from your troops?

CPT Schack: [pauses] I guess most of us already knew this, but it was definitely reinforced: I learned that if you give someone a task and a reason to do it and you provide some resources, the troops will do just about anything—and surprise you at their creativity in doing it.

If, say, your own eighteen-year-old son or daughter wanted to join the military, what would you tell him or her?

CPT Schack: Serving in the military is one of the only jobs where you're part of something larger than yourself, a job that has a moral and just cause to it. It's not about making money. Whether you're in for three years or twenty years, whether you enjoy yourself or not, you'll ultimately come out a better person.

Nathan Olson

ABOVE:
Captain Eric Schack
Company Commander
Hometown: DePere

First Sergeant
David Christiansen
Hometown: Oshkosh

First Lieutenant
Bradley Bucher
Executive Officer
Hometown: Green Bay

LEFT:
Captain Eric Schack
addresses a group of
C Company soldiers.

Joseph Streeter

INTERVIEW WITH FIRST SERGEANT DAVID CHRISTIANSON

This was a mission where the young leaders, the sergeants and staff sergeants, had most of the responsibility out there on the road. What does that mean to you?

1SG Christianson: It means that my team leaders and squad leaders needed to be ready to perform all missions assigned to them without guidance from their platoon leaders or platoon sergeants.

What one skill, more than any other, makes a leader excellent?

1SG Christianson: The ability to listen to what their subordinates are saying and then to be flexible in making plans to accommodate what's really happening. Two minutes into any plan it's all gone out the window, anyway.

How important is military bearing?

1SG Christianson: Very important. It's not only your unit that looks at you but other units too—Marines, sailors, airmen. Your bearing alone can give an impression about your unit and about how disciplined you are.

As the most senior and experienced soldier in your company, how has your career prepared you for this deployment?

1SG Christianson: As a first sergeant, my job over here is pretty similar to what it was back home: soldier caring. Making sure they have everything they need and instilling discipline within the unit. Making sure the subordinates at the lowest level get all the supplies and information they need to accomplish the mission.

Headquarters Company "Hellhounds"

INTERVIEW WITH MAJOR MATTHEW STORMS

What was the toughest moment for you on this deployment?

MAJ Storms: When Staff Sergeant Cox's vehicle was hit by an IED, we were sitting back here [at Camp Navistar], not knowing what was going on. They [Cox, Shropshire, and 1SG Krzanowski, who was the driver for the mission] requested a medevac, a helicopter to transport their wounded. But we didn't get much more information for a while. It was really tough not knowing and not being able to do anything to help.

What was the best moment?

MAJ Storms: When are we getting on the plane? [laughs] Not sure if it's a single best moment but many moments: watching young officers and NCOs come into their own, grow, learn, improve, become competent in their technical responsibilities and become better leaders. There are particular moments when those things become evident to the soldiers. Those moments are special. For example, when a specialist who initially struggled as a gunner [but] by the end of the deployment [has] stepped up and is commanding his own vehicle. That growth is awesome to observe.

What have you learned from your troops?

MAJ Storms: Perspective. Making sure I take care of the things that matter and developing a sense for when to let things slide.

If, say, your own eighteen-year-old son or daughter wanted to join the military, what would you tell him or her?

MAJ Storms: I do have a fourteen-year-old daughter. I'd tell her for a lot of people the military is a great way to start your adulthood, learning the importance of leadership, responsibility, and values. It's for some people and not for others. If my daughter was really interested I'd encourage her, but I wouldn't push her. It depends on the personality and interests of the person.

Nathan Olson

First Sergeant
Darren Krzanowski
Hometown: Mosinee

Major Matthew Storms
Company Commander
Hometown: Madison

INTERVIEW WITH FIRST SERGEANT DARREN KRZANOWSKI

This was a mission where the young leaders, the sergeants and staff sergeants, had most of the responsibility out there on the road. What does that mean to you?

Joseph Streeter

1SG Krzanowski: It means that the young leaders stepped up and took care of business. We saw a lot of growth over this year. For example, all of our teams who went on the road doing the security escort mission were noncombat arms—cooks, fuelers, supply guys. They ran missions [as well as] or better than the infantry guys. I'm proud of them for that.

What one skill, more than any other, makes a leader excellent?

1SG Krzanowski: You need to be their friend but not their pal. It's a matter of separating yourself and knowing when and how to separate yourself. As part of a team, you need to be able to be their friend, to hang out. But you also need to be able to make decisions that put them at risk.

How important is military bearing?

1SG Krzanowski: Is that a part on a tank? [laughs] It's very important. When everything else fails it's what you go back to, instincts brought about through training.

As one of the most senior and experienced soldiers in your company, how has your career prepared you for this deployment?

1SG Krzanowski: Basic soldier caring doesn't change, no matter what mission you're on. We went from infantry to convoy escort, but the soldier caring stayed the same. Learning that was the most important thing for me.

The battalion assembles for an awards ceremony.

RIGHT:
Major Aponte didn't spend much time in his tent, but when he did everything was within an arm's reach.

BELOW RIGHT:
Drawings from grandchildren and a valentine from his wife testify to the strength of Major Aponte's family.

INTERVIEW
Major David Aponte

While it's true that most of the soldiers in the 2-127th fit a profile—young, in college or planning on going to college, from small town Wisconsin—we did have a few elder statesmen.

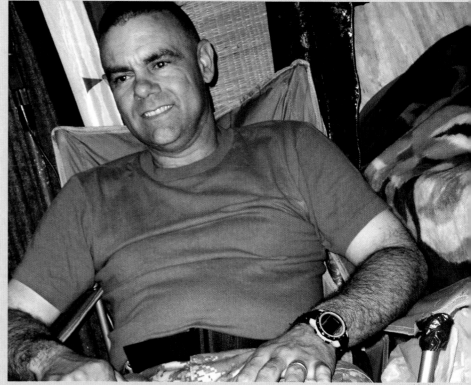

Benjamin Buchholz

Major David Aponte, from La Crosse, was the battalion S4, the staff officer in charge of supply and logistics. He's also got a brood of children and grandchildren back home that seemed to increase in number as the deployment lengthened. During the interview Major Aponte ticked them off on his fingers: his wife, Joan (whose cake has twenty-nine candles on it every year); Chrystal, also twenty-nine; Jim, twenty-eight; twins Cazzie and Arial, twenty-six; Kristen, twenty-five; and grandkids Arson (eight), Lexy (seven), Josh (four), Sadie (four), Abigail (two), Zach (one), and Anthony, who was born shortly after we arrived in Kuwait.

Major Aponte truly is a father figure for the battalion.

What do you miss about home?

MAJ Aponte: I miss the routine of walking my dogs, the morning walk to work, cross-country skiing. Once I woke up here and heard rain and thought it was a river like the Mississippi at home. I miss doing a lot of camping and canoeing. I spend most summers in the Boundary Waters and am called the "Wild One" back home. Probably every weekend we go camping somewhere. I'm looking forward to taking the grandkids camping next year. I miss snow.

Benjamin Buchholz

How has your perception of home changed since coming here?

MAJ Aponte: Regular day-to-day home things seem more valuable. You're also limited here in leaving post. You just can't go and wander around like I like to do. I miss my wife.

How do you like living communally in the tents? Do your tentmates have any strange habits?

MAJ Aponte: I spend very little time in my tent, but when I am there I have things set up so I can reach everything in my tent space: coffee, music. I don't like having to get up and walk to the latrine to pee so I've got a pee bottle I keep under the bed. I think the small space here is getting me ready for the nursing home.

Sometimes coming into the dark tent from the bright sun I run into people. That is strange. I hardly know if anyone is around. We're all very quiet in this tent. I'm also usually the first one to sleep, around 9 o'clock, and the first one up, around 5 in the morning. I start coffee and go for a walk around the perimeter of the camp. At home I'm up by 4:15 every day to walk the dogs.

Benjamin Buchholz

ABOVE:
Major Aponte's headgear, retired for the day.

LEFT:
As Major Aponte's tentmate throughout the deployment, I thought the sound of trickling water was his coffeemaker starting up in the wee hours of the morning. How wrong I was!

Benjamin Buchholz

Benjamin Buchholz

ABOVE:

Some soldiers were able to add quite a few amenities to their bunk spaces: TVs, DVD players, even video game consoles.

RIGHT:

Photos of family and Musil's new girlfriend along with enough cappuccino to OD the whole battalion.

INTERVIEW
Sergeant First Class Michael Musil

Being apart from loved ones, from family, is one of the toughest things in a deployment. It's difficult from both sides of the equation, for the soldier and for the family. Every military family feels the pangs of this separation. And every family copes in its own way.

Sergeant First Class Musil faced one of the most difficult family challenges of any of our soldiers while deployed. His three daughters, Elaine, Michelle, and Samantha, were thirteen, fifteen, and seventeen when he deployed, a tough stage for any father, let alone a father away fighting a war.

Complicating this, Musil and his wife had divorced about a year before the deployment, and Musil had started a serious relationship with a woman who had children of her own. They were making plans to merge their families, possibly to get married, just before he learned about the deployment. Musil had to rely on email and the few phone calls he could make to hold things together.

What do you miss about home?

SFC Musil: I miss playing video games with my daughter Lainey. We used to play a lot. I get déjà vu sometimes coming back to my tent after missions because I get swarmed by the younger soldiers—just like getting swarmed by my children when I come home from work.

Benjamin Buchholz

Benjamin Buchholz

Sergeant First Class Musil emails his girlfriend, Tracy, in his bunk area. Internet service in our tents established an important link home and allowed soldiers to conduct private, personal business that they might not have felt comfortable conducting in a group setting in the Morale, Wellfare, and Recreation tent.

How has your perception of home changed since coming here?

SFC Musil: Life here is almost identical. Issues with the Joes are like issues with the kids back home. From 8:30 until 10:00 at night are my quiet hours, just like home.

How do you like living communally in the tents? Do your tentmates have any strange habits?

SFC Musil: Stevens is mostly deaf, so he listens to his TV way too loud and falls asleep to it. Padgett is a hermit; his light is on all the time so you never know when he's sleeping. I can tell when Boutott needs attention because he laughs aloud when watching TV. And Groll has sort of a college lifestyle, guys always coming by to look for him and hang out.

Teenagers can be relied upon to produce some interesting angst-ridden art, like this example hanging in a place of honor on Sergeant First Class Musil's locker.

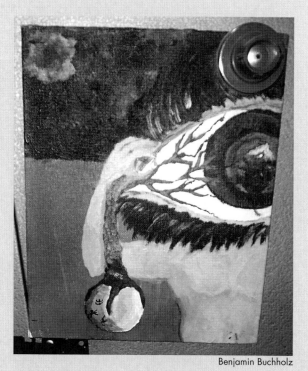

Benjamin Buchholz

Email can never replace being at home at critical times in the lives of our families. Nor does email allow the sort of conversation, the give-and-take, necessary to resolve difficult situations, especially since during missions we couldn't respond immediately. Email might sit for days without being answered. Yet it kept us in touch with loved ones in a way that soldiers of other wars could not have imagined. The following are excerpts from emails between Sergeant First Class Musil and Lainey, his youngest daughter.

----- Original Message -----
From: lainey musil <emailaddress@hotmail.com>
Date: Saturday, December 17, 2005 1:54 am
Subject: RE: Hi again
Hey dad,
. . . Yeah you're right it would be easier if they did live with us but we might not have our own personal space. . . . Just wish you could come home already and we could just leave everything the way it was 3 years ago. Even though you and mom weren't happy doesn't mean we weren't happy. Dad I do hope that you don't get mad. This is just weird with everyone dating and all that crap but I don't know it's confusing. And I can't really say it. I can more think it than say it in words or an email. But when I do know how to explain you'll be the first I tell. I hope you know how I feel
love you dad
lainey

From: <SFC.MUSILemail@us.army.mil>
To: lainey musil <emailaddress@hotmail.com>
Subject: Re: RE: Hi again
Date: Sun, 18 Dec 2005 08:42:21 +0300

Hi Lainey,
I am glad you told me how you feel. I am not going to tell you to learn to deal with it, because that's not the right thing to do. But I am going to try and persuade you to see it how I see it. And I think it is going to be hard to do. . . . Tracy knows that you guys like your time and space with me and will do her best to make sure that you do.

Interview: Sergeant Michael Musil

It's impossible to turn back time to three years ago. It's a little selfish to want someone to be totally, 100% unhappy just so that you can be happy. . . . A good person finds a way to make as many people happy as they can without worrying about themselves (that's a little deep but true). I try to make everyone happy if I can. I am trying to do that now but it has become very hard. We will still have everything we did and still do everything that we have always done. But we would just have roommates and would have to learn to share. . . .

I think Tracy is alot like me. She tries to make everyone around her happy and not worry about herself. That's why it is so easy for me to like her. And I can't help liking her which is why I am writing all of this. I think and hope that if we try this and everybody gets settled (which won't happen overnight), it will be like it was. I think even better. Me and you will still have our time, I promise. I miss it too. We will just have to share sometimes.

I hope I am making sense. Let me know what you think.

Love always, Dad.

----- Original Message -----
From: lainey musil <emailaddress@hotmail.com>
Date: Saturday, December 17, 2005 1:54 am
Subject: RE: re: RE: Hi again

Hey dad,

Thanks for understanding. I was thinking that you were going to take it the wrong way. Thanks for not telling me to accept it or deal with it. . . . Yeah I really do hope that this all works out and yeah no one is going to get used to it over night. Just it will be weird when we all live together because then your going to have to share all your time with me sam chelle david angela robin tracy and your self. And not just the 4 of us. But yeah I will learn to accept it. (I hate that word lol) Just I don't know just you not being here makes it all weird. Cuz when we visit mom we can call you and tell us our problems and now look I'm giving you an email that takes you about 4 days until you read it. But it's okay at least I get to talk to you. Every one says hi. Did you hear that Robin like cut all her hair off its like up to her ear. I don't like it at all. Sorry got off the subject. . . . Yeah it would be selfish to rewind 3 years and make it all good again. But I understand. . . .

I'm sorry. But I have to go. I understand what your all talking about though. MERRY CHRISTMAS. Your gift should be coming soon.

Love you dad

Lainey

Nathan Olson

CHAPTER 4

Staff and Logistics

Sending teams of soldiers into a hostile environment requires a tremendous amount of behind-the-scenes support and planning.

The Army system organizes that work into functional areas and assigns teams, or staff sections, to become experts. Staff sections advise the unit commander in each of six functional areas: S1: personnel, administration, and medical; S2: intelligence; S3: operations; S4: logistics and maintenance; S5: civil affairs and public affairs; S6: communications. At higher echelons of command the staff becomes more and more specialized. At the battalion level, though, each member of the staff covers a wide range of tasks in order to provide across-the-board services to our war-fighters, enabling them to more easily and expertly do the three things that make missions successful: shoot, move, and communicate.

Ultimately all these functional areas—everything the battalion does or fails to do—is the responsibility of the battalion commander. However, the battalion commander's executive officer, or XO, coordinates and supervises the staff.

Connexes (huge metal shipping containers) are moved, sorted, and loaded for the return home, all of them full of gear we used on the deployment.

Joseph Streeter

Nathan Olson

Joseph Streeter

ABOVE:

Lieutenant Allah, an Iraqi police officer with whom our battalion worked, helped us pay reparations to Iraqis for damage our convoys caused and to curb the semi hijacking incidents in Safwan.

ABOVE CENTER:

Sergeant Jesse Fenske repairs a Humvee.

ABOVE RIGHT:

The maintenance tents at sunset.

Nathan Olson

The battalion staff, left to right: Lieutenant Colonel (Chaplain) Andrew Aquino, S6 Captain Dan Nowacki, S4 Major David Aponte, S2 Captain Frank Lovine, S3 Major John Oakley, EWO Lieutenant (Navy) Epi Atencio, XO Major Thomas O'Brien, Physician Assistant Lieutenant Shawn Murphy, S5 Captain Benjamin Buchholz, S1 Captain Walter Neta.

Photograph contributed by
a member of the 2-127th

Benjamin Buchholz

Joseph Streeter

ABOVE LEFT:

Our medics treated a huge variety of disorders and injuries, from post-traumatic stress disorder (PTSD) to sprained ankles to emergency tracheotomies. They practiced between missions using dummies and theatre-grade wound simulators called moulage kits.

ABOVE CENTER:

Sergeant Abe Lewis, trained as a combat lifesaver, treats an Iraqi man who was injured in a vehicle accident.

ABOVE RIGHT:

Captain Walter Neta, Sergeant Charles Hobbs, and Specialist Trevor Anderson from the S1 Section organize awards prior to a ceremony.

LEFT:

Doc Van Heuklon was a combat medic, one of the battalion's many specialized functions.

S1 Section: Personnel, Administration, and Medical

Led by Captain Walter Neta, who served as a Marine in the first Gulf War and served one tour in Operation Iraqi Freedom with the 724th Engineer Battalion, also from Wisconsin, our S1 Section staff comprised seven personnel. S1 responsibilities include tracking personnel status; publishing administrative rules and regulations; reviewing, routing, and approving official personnel actions, such as awards and soldier performance evaluation reports; conducting legal liaison with staff judge advocate advisors from our higher headquarters; managing mid-tour leave (our two weeks of vacation) and emergency leave; tracking injured or ill soldiers; and distributing mail.

The S1 Section also manages the battalion medical section, which fielded eighteen combat medics to the line companies. These medics went on missions just like regular soldiers, but because of their special training and skills, they were led by First Lieutenant Shawn Murphy, the battalion physician assistant.

The sheer number of teams on the road prevented us from having a combat medic for every mission. For this reason, the medical section trained almost every soldier in the battalion as combat lifesavers, teaching them basic lifesaving skills including starting an emergency IV, putting on a tourniquet, stopping bleeding, and treating for trauma and shock. In addition to these combat duties, the medics managed unit health records and provided assessments to the battalion commander on the state of medical readiness.

More than half of our medics received their Combat Medical Badges for treating wounded soldiers while in contact with the enemy. Our medics were an asset to more than just our battalion. One received a Bronze Star for cumulatively helping more than thirty civilians and coalition forces.

Photograph contributed by
a member of the 2-127th

Nathan Olson

Captain Iovine briefs the commander.

S2 Section: Intelligence

The old joke about "military intelligence" being an oxymoron certainly doesn't apply at combat unit level, where assessing the enemy's capabilities and trying to predict his most likely and most dangerous courses of action often saves the lives of soldiers and contributes to the success of the mission.

Unlike the small city–sized area of operation in which most infantry battalions work, our mission spanned all the roads, all the danger areas in Iraq. Thus our S2 Section, led by Captain Frank Iovine (a police officer and member of Kenosha's SWAT team), analyzed and provided continuously updated information to our soldiers for the entire theater of war.

While most S2 work is graphic in nature—charting trends, providing up-to-date maps that show enemy tendencies and critical locations, developing schematics to help soldiers and leadership visualize enemy procedures—these products are classified and cannot be shared.

The 2-127th's S2 staff consisted of six personnel. Their job sifting and winnowing reports and statistics often wasn't glamorous, but they provided a service critical to every mission. And they were always in the know.

S3 Section: Operations

The 2-127th operations cell, led by Major John Oakley and Sergeant Major John Schiermeister, planned missions, assessed past missions to glean recommendations for future improvements, and provided command and control for the ongoing battle. Each of the three line companies also had its own company-level operations staff, responsible for implementing battalion plans and passing feedback from the crews up to the battalion staff.

These three functions—planning, assessment, and battle command—were the responsibility of twelve personnel working round-the-clock shifts, along with another three personnel in each company ops cell.

The S3 Section's job was to turn the commander's vision into action and to assess and recommend changes based on the shifting focus of missions. As with the S2 Section, many of the materials the S3 Section used and produced are classified.

The S3 Section conducted its operations from the Tactical Operations Center, or the TOC, at Camp Navistar. The TOC, a double-wide air-conditioned trailer, was like a brain center for the battalion. The S3 also maintained a forward element, along with maintenance and communications personnel, at CSC Cedar II, the first base north of Navistar. Many of our missions stopped at Cedar, making it essential to provide on-demand leadership and services there to fix problems.

Nathan Olson

LEFT:
Major Oakley, Sergeant Major Schiermeister, and Captain Paul Potamianos from the S3 Section discuss plans.

ABOVE:
The forward S3 element at Cedar.

Nathan Olson

Nathan Olson

S4 Section: Logistics and Maintenance

A battalion of 620 soldiers with 150 Humvees requires an extensive amount of material to keep the work going—everything from fuel to new uniforms to ammunition to spare vehicle parts. The S4 Section ordered, transported, and distributed all of this, keeping account of it as the soldiers carried it with them or consumed it.

Like the S3 Section, the supply and logistics staff had company-level counterparts, the company supply sergeants and unit armorers. Major David Aponte, a teacher from La Crosse, led the 127th's S4 Section.

Specific S4 supply tasks include shipping the battalion's equipment from the United States to our base in Kuwait and then back at the end of our tour of duty; fielding new test equipment, including water-cooled vests for guntruck crews, improved body armor, better armor for the Humvees, and electronic countermeasures for defeating improvised explosive devices (IEDs); managing a fleet of SUVs for transportation in Kuwait; conducting financial investigations on property lost or damaged during battle; ordering and accounting for ammunition; ordering replacement equipment when soldiers wear out uniforms or other items; and locally purchasing equipment not available through the Army supply system.

One of the 2-127th's biggest success stories was the performance of our battalion maintenance staff. With more than 150 trucks on the road, the maintenance staff of forty-two personnel, led by Chief Warrant Officer Todd Jeno, kept busy the entire year.

Our predecessors in Iraq, using the same equipment and the same vehicles, generally had fifteen or more vehicles inoperable at any given time. Chief Jeno kept it to only two or three under repair at any one time, and for long stretches every truck was fully

ABOVE:

Chief Jeno, our battalion maintenance officer, watches as several of his men receive awards.

RIGHT:

Staff Sergeant David Kavanaugh, a supply sergeant, inspects items being shipped home at the end of the tour.

Nathan Olson

Sergeant Jesse Fenske works on a guntruck's suspension.

operational, an amazing achievement. Our battalion *never* refused a mission and always had a reserve of several vehicles waiting for the next order.

In addition to keeping the trucks on the road, Chief Jeno's crews installed new armor kits and a plethora of other devices on the Humvees, often customizing the interiors to move the many pieces of electronic equipment into the location each vehicle commander preferred.

The fielding of new equipment usually occurred at Camp Arifjan, the main U.S. base located farther south in Kuwait than Camp Navistar. Thanks to our maintenance section's expertise, the crews were able to install most new equipment right at Navistar, reducing the time required and keeping more guntrucks on the road and in the fight.

RIGHT:

Our battalion's Family Readiness Group donated school supplies and other items for Iraqi children. Here Specialist Lamond Hill and Sergeant Ryan Sanders fill a crate for delivery to Safwan. Our Family Readiness Group provided about thirty such crates of crayons, markers, glue, pencils, and even shoes to schoolchildren in Safwan and other locations.

BELOW RIGHT:

Captain Benjamin Buchholz (in gray uniform at far right) and British soldiers meet with the president of the town council in Safwan.

S5 Section: Civil Affairs and Public Affairs

The 2-127th's smallest staff section, civil and public affairs operations, was really a one-man show. I was selected to serve as the S5 because I knew some Arabic and because I had worked in marketing and public affairs prior to returning to active duty as the battalion's full-time training officer. My duties included meeting with local Iraqi authorities, advising the battalion commander about our mission's impact on Iraqi recon-

Joseph Streeter

struction and self-governance, conducting liaison with British and Danish forces in the area, writing press releases, escorting visiting media, and assisting the Family Readiness Group back in Wisconsin in its efforts to take care of soldiers and family members.

Joseph Streeter

S6 Section: Communications

The 2-127th's communications section, led by Captain Dan Nowacki and Sergeant First Class Vital Silva, ensured that our soldiers were trained to operate all the sophisticated electronics found on today's battlefield. They also maintained that equipment.

Staff Sergeant David Loeffler and Specialist Wesley Pompa work on a Humvee's MTS system.

Nathan Olson

Joseph Streeter

Nathan Olson

ABOVE LEFT:
The inside of the Humvee is crammed with communications equipment.

ABOVE RIGHT:
Sergeant First Class Tim Lease conducts a commo check before a mission. He checks all the equipment to ensure it is functioning and then calls the battalion Tactical Operations Center and each of the military vehicles in his convoy in turn.

Our battalion served as the communications experts for our brigade and for the other units we escorted into Iraq, and our S6 staff mastered a myriad of gear, including MTS, an onboard computer and map-enabled tracking and email system; global positioning system (GPS); SINCGARs, the encrypted radio (usually two per vehicle to allow monitoring of multiple radio networks simultaneously); and electronic IED countermeasures. Our team leaders and soldiers on missions often taught other soldiers how to use equipment or troubleshoot gear that didn't seem to be working. This expertise is directly attributable to the coaching and mentoring done by our communications section, which included thirteen personnel who worked in shifts around the clock.

Joseph Streeter

Three Humvees carrying commo personnel climb Safwan Hill to set up a radio retrans antenna. A retrans station broadcasts a radio signal to a wider area than any single Humvee-mounted antenna could manage on its own. After placing this antenna on the hill the battalion TOC could speak directly to convoys 30 miles away.

INTERVIEW
Specialist Anthony Warigi

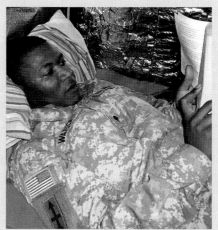

Benjamin Buchholz

The 2-127th brought diverse backgrounds and skills to Iraq. Perhaps no soldier in our battalion better exemplifies this range of skills and life experiences than thirty-three-year-old Specialist Anthony Warigi.

Specialist Warigi immigrated from Kenya to the United States on July 4, 1994, and joined the National Guard in 2002. He is currently studying business and economics at the University of Wisconsin–Oshkosh and hopes to join the United Nations after graduation, working for a specialized agency like UNICEF or UNESCO. He speaks English, French, Swahili, Sheng, and his native tongue, Kikuyu.

Specialist Warigi obtained his U.S. citizenship in spring 2006 while at war, a fitting time and place to reach his long-cherished goal.

RIGHT:
Specialist Warigi studies his UN manual on his bunk. (He walled himself off for privacy with reflective thermal blankets.)

BELOW:
Specialist Warigi keeps a globe nearby to remind him where he is and where he was.

Tell me about your family.

SPC Warigi: I'm the second boy in a family of eight. Two of them, Gabriel and Elizabeth, are also in the USA, but the rest of my family is still in Kenya. I married Emily Taylor, a girl from Iowa whose father was in the Navy. I have one daughter, Isabella Wanjiko Warigi. Wanjiko is my mother's name. I call Isabella "Punkin."

Benjamin Buchholz

What special traditions do you have with your family?

SPC Warigi: We visit the "choo-choo" at Sunset Boulevard in Appleton twice a week. I hate it, but Punkin loves it. My wife and I both come from very religious backgrounds, so Easter and singing in church are both very important to us. We're planning to have our families meet but haven't yet, though several of my friends who are in the USA have met my family here. Back in Kenya one tradition is to cook out goat's meat every weekend, with beer, a real delicacy called "nyama choma."

What do you miss about home?

SPC Warigi: My wife's lasagna. She has a way with lasagna! And she'd probably kill me if I didn't say that. But I miss almost all of my life, hard to tell what's more important. I miss music. I'm no match for my wife's singing. I sound like a frog next to her, but I enjoy singing and listening to her sing. There is no way to begin to explain how much I miss my Punkin, her mannerisms, her insights (yes, those five-year-old insights), crying, reading to her, just driving my car and hearing her in the backseat with the daddy-dos.

How do you like living communally in the tents?

SPC Warigi: I had prepared myself for it. It brings back memories of childhood days fighting for bed space, sometimes four per bed in Kenya plus any friends who are visiting. More if it is raining, because then anyone in the neighborhood comes in and sleeps, friends, family, whomever. We'd put a nylon tarp over our bed to keep the rain off because the roofs were leaky. Soldiers here have both some privacy and some community and camaraderie. For instance, I didn't start with a screen over my bunk, but now I have it mostly so that the guys on night shift aren't interrupted when I'm awake. One of my roommates, Specialist Mooren, snores and leaves his TV on, and I've noticed that the ants like Mooren's section of the tent, probably because of the smell. That's fine by me because then they won't be in my area.

Have you experienced any culture shock since coming over here?

SPC Warigi: Not too much culture shock, but ideology shock, yes. It amazes me how much people are willing to lay claim to beliefs, not that any one system of belief is better than any other but that some people are into religion without free thinking, and despite the negative results. I'm also amazed how culture-oriented the Iraqis and Kuwaitis are, how they think only their society is good. It has brought into sharp focus for me that peace is a necessary ingredient for development. Iraq has resources but no peace, thus the people live in poverty. This makes me want to be part of the United Nations.

Benjamin Buchholz

ABOVE:
Specialist Warigi is a multifaceted guy: St. Paddy and the UN shared space on his bunk.

LEFT:
Specialist Warigi and his daughter, Isabella.

Benjamin Buchholz

Benjamin Buchholz

ABOVE:

Things always come in twos for the Guderskis, like these two A-bags stacked in a corner of Mitch's bunk space.

RIGHT:

In the same company but separate platoons, Mitch and Mike bought walkie-talkies so they could get in touch with each other.

INTERVIEW
Sergeant Mitch Guderski and Sergeant Mike Guderski

In the National Guard you get a lot of family. Even those of us who aren't family often come from the same small towns. We know each other. We've gone fishing at the same "secret" spots. We played the same sports in school. Sometimes we even dated the same girls and didn't realize it until during the deployment, BSing with each other over a game of cards or over the headsets in the Humvee on a mission. It's surprising what you learn about each other.

The Guderski twins are a graphic portrayol of this sameness, this kinship found throughout the battalion. They're sort of famous, like battalion mascots. Everyone has his own "Guderski story."

For instance, as their former company commander I once gave all our troops the afternoon off while we were on a training exercise at Fort McCoy. Both of the Guderskis are bodybuilders, and both were excited for the chance to hit the gym. They thanked me, about ten minutes apart from each other, using the exact same phrasing, the same handshake and salute. To this day I'm not sure if it was two of them thanking me separately or just one of them repeating himself. And although I interviewed the Guderskis separately for this project, their answers were almost identical.

Tell me about your family.

SGT Mitch Guderski: Chris (twenty-nine) was here, he's a captain. He was stationed in Afghanistan, and now he just took a job at Fort McCoy. He visited us on the 26th of September, the same day Wallace and Wendling died, so I'll never forget the day. He was coming back from leave and was able to catch a ride up here during his layover at Ali As-Salem Air Base. We had all three of us brothers in the same tent that night since Mike, my twin, was also here. Tom and Colleen are our par-

Benjamin Buchholz

ents. Sister Kim, twenty-eight. Girlfriend Cassie from Neenah, dating since January. We met online, and the first time I saw her in person was when I was home on leave in the end of May. I was a little skeptical but by the second or third date it was taking off. We've been writing to each other every day, maybe two times a day on email. It's great.

What do you miss about home?

SGT Mike Guderski: Riding my motorcycle and four-wheeler. I've got a Honda 750 Magna. Listening to the radio, being outside at our house in the country, weightlifting, personal free time.

SGT Mitch Guderski: Listening to the radio, 96.9 the Fox, riding four-wheeler, living out in the country, riding motorcycles. I've got a Honda 750 Magna.

Benjamin Buchholz

Benjamin Buchholz

LEFT:
The Guderski twins, Mitch and Mike, or Mike and Mitch. We're not sure who is who. Nor are we quite certain which of them we actually interviewed.

ABOVE:
A pile of letters from Mitch Guderski's new girlfriend.

How has your perception of home changed since being here?

SGT Mike Guderski: It hasn't, really. Getting back home on leave seemed normal, and everything here seems odd still. Even though I still live at home it was nice having no one telling me what to do, where to go. Every day was my own.

How do you like living communally in the tents?

SGT Mitch Guderski: It's alright. Not everyone is on the same mission so everyone does their own thing. Makes sleeping tough sometimes when guys are up and others are trying to sleep. No parties, but always someone to talk to. Coming back from leave depressed me for two days so it was reassuring to talk to everyone and know they felt the same when they came back.

Any funny stories?

SGT Mitch Guderski: I like to impersonate our platoon sergeant, Sergeant First Class Williams, and stomp in to wake everyone up at odd hours. "Get out of the rack, get out of the rack!" But now I think everyone is sick of that joke.

CHAPTER 5

Local Iraqis

Safwan, Iraq: a town of 50,000 people right on the border with Kuwait, a town we called the Tijuana of Iraq because so many riches from Kuwait flowed through its border crossing into Iraq. Safwan's markets flourished and its population almost doubled during the year we were there. New houses and businesses sprang up everywhere, a sign that the economy was recovering and that Iraqis were taking advantage of newfound liberties.

Joseph Streeter

OPPOSITE:
An Iraqi farmer on his tractor stops for one of our guntrucks as a convoy turns the corner in front of him.

LEFT:
Downtown Safwan.

Joseph Streeter

Joseph Streeter

ABOVE:
One of the Iraqis' favorite things to get from our soldiers was water. We kept our bottled water on ice in coolers, so it was a treat to them to have cool, fresh, filtered water.

RIGHT:
Safwan is the main border crossing with rich Kuwait, and we saw signs everywhere of its improving economy.

FAR RIGHT:
Reverse-osmosis drinking water is shipped into Safwan from Basrah and made available at numerous tanks, like this one.

Every day we sent between fifteen and fifty convoys through this town. Doing so required a lot of coordination with town officials, and it allowed us the opportunity to get to know some local people, to see how the Iraqis live.

In the deep south almost all Iraqis are Shi'a, repressed for several decades by Saddam Hussein. They've seen war their entire lives—some of the major battles in the Iran-Iraq war in the 1980s took place just a few miles to the east; the treaty for Operation Desert Storm was signed at an airfield a few miles to the west; the bulk of U.S. and coalition forces rolled right through this town on their way north to Baghdad at the beginning of Operation Iraqi Freedom.

As we interviewed and photographed Iraqis during civil affairs missions—business owners, policemen, average citizens—we were reminded again and again that we must be thankful for the liberties we have at home. Such things are not universal.

In Safwan policing organizations vie for supremacy and do not support local ordinances or the elected town council. Tribal and religious loyalties trump elected leadership. Graft and nepotism are rampant, while women's rights pale in comparison to what we've come to expect in western society. Still, despite these obstacles, Safwan's town council moved forward, gradually exerting itself more and more throughout the year we were there, encouraged by the British unit responsible for the town and working with us to mediate any issues related to our mission of moving convoys through the city.

Joseph Streeter

Joseph Streeter

Joseph Streeter

Joseph Streeter

Joseph Streeter

LEFT:
Transportation for Iraqis is catch-as-catch can. Often our teams would report suspicious individuals waiting under highway overpasses— until we found out it was the traditional bus stop! Anyone with room in his car will pick up travelers for a small fee.

BELOW LEFT:
This alley outside the Safwan police headquarters building was familiar terrain for our teams due to weekly and sometimes daily meetings we attended. The Safwan police hauled cars here to form a barricade around their front entrance. Any car they impounded would end up here, at least until the owner paid for its release.

BELOW RIGHT:
A town council member and a major from the Iraqi police from Safwan in a discussion at the Safwan police headquarters building.

RIGHT:

A female teenager with a baby (a little sister?) showed up at Hussein Khazim's shop. The girl declined to be photographed, so Hussein held the baby for the camera. The baby's name was Mona.

BELOW:

Hussein Khazim shows a customer the wares in his shop on a busy corner in Safwan.

INTERVIEW WITH HUSSEIN KHAZIM

Age: sixteen

Occupation: merchant, salesman at his father's "Seven-Eleven" shack in Safwan

Education: completed sixth grade

Hussein Khazim's father, Khazim Abu Saleh, is a retired police officer with no pension or retirement pay; he has owned the Seven-Eleven shop for thirteen years. Hussein is one of eleven children (four boys and seven girls) and is the only one who works. Born in 1956, Khazim has lived in Safwan since 1967. He told us Safwan was a good place in the 1980s, before the Iran-Iraq war and the two American wars.

Joseph Streeter

What do you think of the United States?

Hussein Khazim: Good people, better than good.

Have you had any interesting experiences with U.S. troops?

Hussein Khazim: Once a convoy from Camp Bucca passed by while I was working in my shop, cutting ice for a customer and drinking a Pepsi. I was laughing with the customer and as a joke I threw my empty Pepsi can at the customer. The convoy thought I was throwing something at them so they arrested me and took me to Umm Qasr to the Iraqi police. They didn't harm me or bother me much. My father picked me up a few hours later, no harm done.

How much do you earn at your shop?

Hussein Khazim: 20,000 Iraqi dinars a week on a bad week, 50,000 on a good week. [1 U.S. dollar = 1,400 Iraqi dinar, so this is about twenty dollars a week]. I sell ice in 12-inch by 8-inch chunks for 750 dinars. And I sell other things too: soda, candy, lightbulbs.

What are your hopes?

Hussein Khazim: Security. Since the U.S. entered Iraq it has been more peaceful. Saddam was bad for southern Iraq, for the Shi'a. I don't want to get married, not yet at least, not until I have enough money to raise a family.

Joseph Streeter

Joseph Streeter

INTERVIEW WITH ABDEL KHAZIM

Age: twenty-seven

Occupation: tomato farmer, makes about 300,000–400,000 Iraqi dinar a year ($250 U.S.) His farm is a few miles north of Safwan, near Az Zubayr.

Education: completed sixth grade We interviewed Abdel while our RSE team searched his car at a checkpoint.

Abdel Khazim answers questions while members of the 2-127th's Route Security Element search his car.

How many times have you been stopped at U.S. checkpoints before?

Abdel Khazim: Never.

What do you think about being stopped here?

Abdel Khazim: Feels like I am suspected. I think you are looking for bombs.

What do you think of the United States?

Abdel Khazim: I think the U.S. controls everything and makes Iraq better and safer because Iraq needs control right now. The U.S. is a good asset to the Iraqis. I think the U.S. will be in Iraq for three to four more years.

What are your hopes for the future?

Abdel Khazim: I hope the economy will be better and the country will be safer.

What do you do for fun?

Abdel Khazim: [embarrassed] Not much, maybe just sit and chill out and visit neighbors.

Abu Saleh's Army T-shirt caught our attention as we moved through the market. We decided to stop and interview him.

Joseph Streeter

INTERVIEW WITH HABEEB ABU SALEH

Age: seventeen

Occupation: welder and blacksmith in Safwan, earning 5,000 to 6,000 Iraqi dinar per day (about $4 U.S.)

Family: twelve brothers and sisters

Habeeb just got married and doesn't have children yet. He said that business is slow but that it is good to be working at all.

Have you ever met any U.S. troops before?

Habeeb Abu Saleh: No. Never. This is the first time.

How did you get the T-shirt, then?

Habeeb Abu Saleh: From in the market.

What do you think about the U.S. and British presence here?

Habeeb Abu Saleh: It is good that they are here to help Iraqis and get rid of Saddam. Saddam was a dog and the son of a dog.

What are your hopes for the future?

Habeeb Abu Saleh: Security, stability, better business, electricity all the time, more tools, more customers for the blacksmith business. I need a good source of oxygen in order to weld better, and more workshop space, but this is enough to start. I weld gates, windows, fix things. The iron is still too expensive, especially the good stuff for gates. Two meters of iron is 20,000 dinar.

Is Western culture—cell phones and movies and music—a good thing for Iraq?

Habeeb Abu Saleh: American movies are fun and the best in the world but too free and open for Islam, against our morals. It is a good phenomenon, though, to see how other people live in the world. I watch news and sports on satellite TV.

Who is your favorite actress?

Habeeb Abu Saleh: Nur al-Shareef, the Egyptian. [Someone in the crowd teases him, says he wants to marry Nur al-Shareef.]

Joseph Streeter

A disabled boy who helps at Abu Saleh's shop.

The ice slides off the ice machine in big blocks at Ayyad Muyahee's factory near Safwan. This new ice plant is clean and modern-looking. The old plant, on the other side of town, looked highly unsanitary.

Joseph Streeter

INTERVIEW WITH AYYAD MUYAHEE

Age: thirty

Occupation: ice factory owner; the plant is one mile north of Safwan on the main road to Basra city and produces one thousand blocks of ice each day.

Family: fourteen brothers and sisters, four children of his own

You've built a new ice factory here. Perfect timing, too, with summer just about to start. How did you come up with the money for this?

Ayyad Muyahee: It cost 300 million Iraqi dinar [$200,000 U.S.] to build. I expect it will take three to five years to earn my investment back. I sell each block of ice for 1,000 dinar. I used to be an electrician until I arranged for some business partners from Nasiriyah to help me open this factory.

How do you feel about the United States being here?

Ayyad Muyahee: Comfortable, no problems with them. I think the U.S. will be here five more years.

Joseph Streeter

Joseph Streeter

LEFT:
Ayyad Muyahee's employees transport the ice on trucks to stores around town, where it is cut and sold.

ABOVE:
Some enterprising vendors, like this boy, sell the ice from wheelbarrows.

BELOW LEFT:
Capitalism is alive and well in Iraq. Whenever our convoys stopped, merchants appeared, trying to sell us Viagra, knives, cigarettes, and movies.

BELOW RIGHT:
New meets old: a camel herder with nice shades and a cell phone.

Joseph Streeter

Joseph Streeter

97

Joseph Streeter

ABOVE:
Ayat Abu Ahmed's garden.

RIGHT:
Captain Buchholz interviews Abu Ahmed outside his father's house on the outskirts of Safwan.

INTERVIEW WITH AYAT ABU AHMED

Age: thirty
Occupation: tradesman importing cement from Kuwait, earning about 1,000,000 Iraqi dinar a year ($700 U.S.)
Education: completed intermediate school (middle school)
Family: two sons, Ahmed, age three, and Nassar, age six; other family members, including Ayat Abu Ahmed's father, live in the same house, though it would have been impolite to ask about them.

Joseph Streeter

Have you met any U.S. troops before?

Ayat Abu Ahmed: Yes, last year my son Ahmed spilled a pot of boiling water on himself. The U.S. troops got him medical aid and a hospital visit, and now he is healthy. They also brought medicine for my other son, Nassar.

What do you think of U.S. and British personnel being here in Iraq?

Ayat Abu Ahmed: You helped Iraqis get rid of a bad person in Saddam Hussein. Saddam killed my Uncle Shayal during the Iraq-Iran War in the 1980s when Shayal refused to fight.

Any interesting stories about the United States in Safwan?

Ayat Abu Ahmed: When the war started in 2003 some of the convoys going north through Safwan got lost, so I stood on the corner by the bridge and pointed the way to Baghdad for them.

What are your hopes for the future?

Ayat Abu Ahmed: No government like Saddam's government after the U.S. leaves, and justice against Saddam now.

Joseph Streeter

LEFT:
Captain Buchholz (right)
and interpreter Wael
"Willy" Mahmoud speak
with Abu Ahmed outside
his house. Bags of
concrete from Abu
Ahmed's business are
stacked in the shade.

BELOW:
Specialist Reid Jome lets
Nassar look through the
sight of his weapon
while Nassar's brother,
Ahmed, watches in envy.

What do you do for fun?

Ayat Abu Ahmed: I take
my family to Baghdad or
Suleimaniyya. I would also
like to go to America someday.

Who's your favorite movie star?

Ayat Abu Ahmed: The actor
who drove a big truck in the
movie with the time travelers . . .
Arnold Schwarzenegger.

Joseph Streeter

Staff Sergeant David Hottenstine lowers the flag to half-mast.

Nathan Olson

CHAPTER 6

Fallen and Wounded

Our battalion lost three soldiers killed in action: Sergeant Andrew Wallace and Specialist Michael Wendling on September 26, 2005, and Sergeant Ryan Jopek on August 1, 2006. All three died of wounds received from IED blasts while escorting convoys on MSR Tampa, the main supply route from Kuwait to Baghdad. Specialist Stephen Castner also died from an IED blast while training with our unit. He was a soldier from Wisconsin deployed with the 1-121st Field Artillery and was on his first mission in Iraq.

When the blast hit Sergeant Wallace and Specialist Wendling, killing them and wounding the third member of their crew, Specialist Jeremy Roskopf, it reverberated through our battalion and through the families back home with a devastating and sobering effect. No longer was this training or an easy mission, a routine. No longer were deaths a statistic heard distantly on the news. These two were friends, comrades, close as brothers to many in the battalion. We'd been on the ground for less than a month, and everyone, to the man, questioned how many more deaths those months would hold. Fortunately, luck, fate, and good discipline on the part of our soldiers made the next few months casualty-free.

When Sergeant Jopek died we'd already begun training our replacement unit, the 1-121st Field Artillery (also from Wisconsin). In fact, Sergeant Jopek was the only 2-127th soldier in the vehicle. It was supposed to have been his last mission, after which he would have completed his responsibilities training the incoming crew and been on his way home. His death was an absolute tragedy.

Sergeant Wallace, Specialist Wendling, and Specialist Roskopf at Camp Shelby.

Photograph contributed by a member of the 2-127th

The healing process—a process that still isn't complete and probably never will be—was a highly personal one. Many soldiers sought comfort talking to the chaplain, talking on the phone to people at home, talking to each other. Friends of these fallen soldiers had to organize, pack, and prepare the personal effects and equipment that Wallace, Wendling, and Jopek had accumulated in their bunk areas. We held memorial services at Camp Navistar even as families back home held their own services. The customary memorial—a soldier's boots, rifle turned upside-down, dog tags—were displayed in front of a podium where friends and generals alike paid their respect.

Brothers Wallace and Wendling

By Brigadier General Charles J. Barr, Commander 143rd Transportation Command (Forward) and Captain Noah Brusky

'Twas a black flag day throughout Navistar Camp,
But not because of the wet bulb temp.

Two young men from Wisconsin's Infantry
Were killed in ground combat by an IED.

2-127th Infantry has seen ground combat before,
Regimental colors bear many streamers of war.

Civil War, The Great War and World War Two,
Heroes to their colors have not been few.

These men stand together like kinfolk recurring,
Reflecting past generations with resolve enduring.

Some have veteran forefathers, uncles and kin,
A few "Les Terribles" Soldiers are serving in war again.

Vietnam, Just Cause, OIF and Desert Storm,
Right sleeve combat patches are proudly worn.

Their loss a burden you bear on broad shoulders,
SGT Wallace, SPC Wendling, proud Infantry Soldiers.

And what of these men will we remember them for?
And how will we honor their sacrifice in war?

Joseph Streeter

We remember that they represent Wisconsin's best,
America's finest Soldiers, CIBs on their chests.

Andrew Wallace and Mike Wendling—your names we repeat,
Strike Forward missions continue amid danger and heat.

May in word and deed your names we always remember,
As we pause and pray each twenty-sixth of September.

Your rifles, Kevlar and dog tags displayed with care,
Three volleys of rifles fire pierce the hot desert air.

And as the somber notes of "Taps" the bugle surrenders,
Saying, "Farewell Brothers Wallace and Wendling, our salutes we render."

These stickers commemorating Sergeant Wallace and Specialist Wendling adorned many of our guntrucks for the remainder of our mission.

Sergeant Wallace at Camp Shelby, looking in through the window of a Humvee.

Photograph contributed by a member of the 2-127th

Sergeant Andrew Wallace
KILLED IN ACTION
September 26, 2005

Comments Given in Memoriam, Camp Navistar, September 30, 2005

Sergeant Jake Paulson: I have come to the conclusion that it is not easy to sum up a man's life using a few feeble words strung together in paragraphs. It is even harder when you went to high school with him and attended the same church growing up. I know I will never do him justice, but I will do my best. Andrew to some, Wally to his friends, and Sergeant Wallace to us here asked me about the National Guard about seven years ago and I told him all about it. Then he consulted his best friend since fourth grade, Dan Kelm, now of Second Platoon, and they chose to join together.

Sergeant Matt Mabee: Kelm and Wally joined the Ripon Unit and from day one were nicknamed

Rusty and Cletus as they went through the ritualistic teasing a private in the Army must go through. Sergeant Paulson here and I are best friends. We grew up in Ripon with Wally and Kelm, who were also best friends. We were all in the same unit. It is easy to remember the pride Andrew showed when he put on his Class A's and did all those color guards we did together. I know Staff Sergeant Doro helped us with those too. All of us are proud to serve our country and had our ups and downs on drill weekends, but Andrew always had a little hint of loving to wear green, even more than the rest of us. No matter what task he had to do or what lame detail he was stuck on, he managed to keep that goofy grin on his face. He always helped out when he knew people needed it, without complaint. He could sometimes go on and on about something and it sometimes made you roll your eyes, but when you think about it, it really did bring a smile to your face, knowing that he really meant well, he was just that kind of a guy, the kind of guy that made you smile and made you laugh. A loveable guy with a big heart.

SGT Paulson: There are a lot of memories I can think of with Wally, and I know Sergeant Kelm has a million more, but I was lucky enough to watch the Packer game this past Sunday with him, the night before the tragedy out on MSR Tampa. That night I had a good chair to sit in to watch the game, and Wally was in a wobbly broken one, so he went and grabbed a water for both of us, so I wouldn't have to lose my seat. Another example of his big heart happened in Mississippi. He stayed instead of going home for his grandmother's funeral because he did not want to miss the GAC [Ground Assault Convoy] training—because he knew it was the most relevant training to the mission and he did not want to miss it. Those examples are a testament to the kind of man he was.

SGT Mabee: Kelm and my convoy were ahead of Andrew's until we got a flat tire. Andrew's convoy passed us and I gave him a wave . . . we saw that Wally had that goofy grin on his face knowing he would beat his friends to Cedar. That same goofy grin he had when we saw him hit his first homerun or when he did something Wallylike at drill. It seems unfortunate for Andrew that he passed us that morning, not knowing what lay ahead, but I know he would not have wanted it any other way. He would have wanted to go through that entrance ramp to Cedar before any of us, if it meant we could live. We just need to keep him and his team's sacrifices in our hearts as we continue forward in this deployment and in life.

SGT Paulson: My dad took a walk with Andrew's step-dad, Joel Brockman, the day after Andrew died, and my dad told me that Joel said Andrew just wanted us to be proud of him. I know there is not a man here today who could say he was not proud of what Andrew did, serving his country because his country asked him to, and for ultimately laying down his life for a cause bigger than himself. All we can do now is carry on our mission, because that is what Andrew and Michael Wendling

Sergeant Wallace at Camp Shelby.

Photograph contributed by a member of the 2-127th

would want us to do. We cannot let our cowardly enemy shake our core values. They want to win by striking fear in our hearts. We need to stand up even taller and let them know you don't mess with men from Wisconsin, men from the United States of America, men who are not afraid to lay down their lives for their country, men like Wally and Wendling.

It is hard to know Wally left behind such a beautiful and loving wife and a caring family. I know Wally was a big family man, and it hurts to know what he has left behind, but I feel a comfort knowing that on Sunday, Wally went to church here at Navistar with his best friend, Dan Kelm. Those of you from the Ripon/Waupun Unit, or "Old Alpha" as we affectionately call it, will understand my humor here.... I just hope God puts Wally through a two-week annual training before letting him into heaven, so he can say he has a full AT under his belt.

Gentlemen, I know we will never be able to hear taps or see an American flag again without thinking of the sacrifices these men gave. We will always remember how brave Andrew and Michael were and how proud we are to say we served with them.

Photograph contributed by a member of the 2-127th

Specialist Michael Wendling
KILLED IN ACTION
September 26, 2005

Bomb in Iraq kills Mayville guardsman; UWM student dies alongside Oshkosh man
by Meg Jones, *Milwaukee Journal Sentinel*, September 27, 2005

The news passed through the stands Monday evening at the Mayville High School JV football game—Michael Wendling, who played on the football, basketball and golf teams and joined the military while still a student, had been killed in Iraq.

Among the words murmured by stunned people as the football game unfolded before them: *explosion, Iraq, Humvee, Mayville.*

"In typical small-town fashion, it had drifted through the town," said Mayville High School Principal Lee Zarnott. "Unfortunately, bad news travels fast."

Wendling, 20, a specialist, was killed Monday with Sgt. Andrew P. Wallace, 25, of Oshkosh when a roadside bomb exploded as they drove past it in Iraq. They were members of Fond du Lac based Charlie Company of the Wisconsin National Guard 2nd Battalion, 127th Infantry Regiment. Their deaths bring to 47 the number of Wisconsin service members killed in Iraq since March 2003.

A high school friend of Wendling's, Spc. Jeremy Roskopf of Brownsville, suffered shrapnel wounds to his legs.

Roskopf and Wendling signed up for the National Guard together while they were in high school. They played on the Mayville golf team, which won the conference championship their senior year.

Wendling, who was on the dean's list at the University of Wisconsin–Milwaukee when his unit was activated, frequently kept in touch with his family via e-mail and talked about what it was like to drive the large, heavy Humvees in Kuwait and Iraq, said his father, Randy Wendling.

"He said they don't go very fast, but he seemed pretty excited about what he was doing," Randy Wendling said in a phone interview Tuesday.

The Appleton-based 2nd Battalion, 127th Infantry Regiment was activated in June and trained at Camp Shelby, Miss. The unit moved to Kuwait in mid-August and has been based in northern Kuwait, providing security to convoys traveling from Kuwait into Iraq, said Wisconsin National Guard Lt. Col. Tim Donovan.

Wendling's father said the roadside bomb hit his son's Humvee near Basra, in southern Iraq. Wendling was the driver, Roskopf was the gunner who stands in the middle of the vehicle and Wallace was the team leader, who normally sits in the front passenger seat.

Randy Wendling said he saw his son shortly before the unit deployed overseas last month. He spent his home leave going to Brewers games, visiting with family and friends and golfing.

His son was upbeat in his e-mails and enjoyed serving in the Wisconsin National Guard, the elder Wendling said.

"He talked about where they were based and what it was like, what they were going to be doing, how hot it was there," said Randy Wendling.

In his last e-mail, received a couple of days before he died, Wendling asked about a care package his family sent him that included bedsheets and beef jerky and told his folks that his company was very busy.

Stu Strook coached Wendling in junior varsity football and golf and remembered a guy who wasn't the most talented athlete but someone who worked hard to improve himself. It was common to see Wendling hitting buckets of golf balls, even after matches, until dark.

"I would call him a grinder. He worked hard. He had a good heart," said Strook.

Wendling also liked to eat. He wasn't fat, so sometimes his teammates wondered where he put all the food. Strook recalled returning from a golf match one day when the team stopped at Burger King. Wendling ordered a Whopper Value Meal with fries and a drink. Nothing unusual about that, except that Wendling went back for four more Whoppers—quarter-pound burgers—and ate them all, to the astonishment of everyone watching him, Strook said.

"Mike was a personality, I guess you would say. He had a great sense of humor. He was a kid who liked to have fun, and kids liked to be around Mike because he was so much fun," said Strook.

Wendling had not declared a major at UWM, but his father said he was leaning toward getting a degree in the sciences. His high school marketing teacher, Rod McSorley, said he thought Wendling would have become an engineer.

Specialist Michael Wendling and his squadmate and friend Specialist Justin Schmidtquist rest between training events at Camp Shelby.

A couple of dozen marketing students from Mayville organized a trip to New York their senior year. The group took in the sights, visited Madison Square Garden and saw *The Lion King* on Broadway. A photo of the group taken on the Staten Island Ferry is pinned to a bulletin board in McSorley's office. McSorley said he was looking at the picture of Wendling and his classmates mugging for the camera as he talked to a reporter Tuesday about his former student.

"When we visited New York, we visited ground zero, and that was important to him. He was close enough to 9-11 to embrace its importance," said McSorley. "He had very good family values. That wouldn't surprise me [that] he had the feeling of giving back."

Photograph contributed by a member of the 2-127th

Sergeant Jopek in the turret of his Humvee.

Photograph contributed by a member of the 2-127th

Sergeant Ryan Jopek
KILLED IN ACTION
August 1, 2006

Comments Given in Memoriam by Sergeant Kyle Clemins, August 8, 2006

I have always thought that a person's true character is shown in the small things they do, our daily activities and interactions with others. Sergeant Jopek was not a superstar recognized for doing spectacular things. He was a simple person with "heart." Jopek put forth an honest effort along with his full attention to whatever he did, including his interaction with others. But before I talk about Jopek's character I have to mention his most memorable characteristic.

If you were to ask anyone who knew Sergeant Jopek, myself included, what is the first thing they picture when they think of him, the answer is almost always the same, his smile. He had a big goofy grin that could brighten the day of anyone he crossed paths with. This truly reflected his character. Jopek was an easygoing person. There was not much life could throw at him that he couldn't just

Photograph contributed by a member of the 2-127th

Photograph contributed by a
member of the 2-127th

LEFT:
**Sergeant Jopek (at top
left) and the guys from
his squad before a
mission.**

ABOVE:
**Sergeant Jopek was
selected from an
appreciative audience to
be feted by the Denver
Bronco Cheerleaders on
stage at Camp Navistar.**

shrug off and let go of. It was because of his easygoing attitude and southern drawl that he earned the nickname Eeyore when we were mobilizing at Camp Shelby.

As the year passed Sergeant Jopek performed his duties as a gunner and was always willing to learn beyond what was required. There were countless times when I found myself having other things to do at the last minute before a mission and I would rely on Jopek to get not only his job done but parts of my job as well. Without fail I knew I could count on him, because he cared about his role and the mission. In fact, probably the most asked question I heard from him was, "When are we gonna go north again?"—followed by, "How come we never get to go to Mosul?" But Jopek's qualities as a soldier were only a small part of his overall character. In my mind what really made him special was the way he treated others.

I would like you all to recall the day the Bronco Cheerleaders came to camp. Despite putting on a show, the ladies served and ate chow with us. On that day, Jopek and two of his buddies went to eat and take pictures with the cheerleaders at the chow hall. When they got their food and were ready to sit down there were two seats available at the table with all the cheerleaders. One of the boys went to sit down with the cheerleaders and asked Jopek to join him. Jopek declined, because it would have left the other soldier sitting by himself. He passed up an opportunity to sit and mingle with beautiful women to instead sit with someone he had spent almost every day with for the last year. To him I'm sure it was not a hard decision to make; others always came before his own desires.

I remember a time when I was feeling a bit down in spirits. I was on the basketball court shooting hoops by myself. Jopek had just gotten done eating chow and was walking back with the rest of his friends. Instead of just walking by he stopped and without saying a word just shot baskets with me. This may seem like such a small incident, but to me it made a world of difference. Jopek had the ability to recognize when someone needed a friend. It was nothing for him to take a little time out of his schedule just to lift the spirits of someone in need.

Sergeant Jopek was without a doubt an enlightened soul. His empathy toward others and his dedication to whatever he put his mind too made him an ideal soldier and a reliable friend. Sergeant Jopek's life came to a close far too soon, but for all of us who knew him he will live on in our hearts and minds.

"Fiddler's Green" is a traditional song of the Cavalry. Seargant Jopek's original unit, the 105th Cavalry, combined with the 32nd Engineer Company to form our A Company for deployment. Spurs, the cavalry hat, and this version of "Fiddler's Green" appeared at Sergeant Jopek's memorial as a fitting tribute.

"Fiddler's Green"

Halfway down the trail to Hell,
In a shady meadow green,
Are the souls of all dead troopers camped
Near a good old time canteen,
And this eternal resting place
Is known as Fiddler's Green.

Marching Past, straight through to Hell,
The Infantry are seen,
Accompanied by the Engineers,
Artillery and Marine,
For none but the shades of Cavalrymen
Dismount at Fiddler's Green.

Though some go curving down the trail
To seek a warmer scene,
No trooper ever gets to Hell
Ere he's emptied his canteen,
And so rides back to drink again
With friends at Fiddler's Green.

And so when man and horse go down
Beneath a saber keen,
Or in a roaring charge or fierce melee
You stop a bullet clean,
And the hostiles come to get your scalp,
Just empty your canteen,...
And wait at Fiddler's Green.

*The purple heart medal,
here pinned on Staff
Sergeant Brent Stelzer.*

Joseph Streeter

Wounded in Action

On August 7, 1782, at his headquarters in Newburgh, New York, General George Washington wrote a General Order that read in part, "The General, ever desirous to cherish virtuous ambition in his soldiers as well as foster and encourage every species of military merit, directs that whenever any singularly meritorious action is performed, the author of it shall be permitted to wear on his facings, over his left breast, the figure of a heart in purple cloth or silk edged with narrow lace or binding. Not only instances of unusual gallantry but also of extraordinary fidelity and essential service in any way shall meet with due reward.... The road to glory in a patriot army and a free country is thus open to all." Only three soldiers are known to have received the original Purple Heart award, and the honor was not awarded again until 1932, when the War Department reintroduced the Purple Heart on the two-hundredth anniversary of Washington's birth. Around that time eligibility for a Purple Heart was expanded to include "a wound which necessitates treatment by a medical officer and which is received in action with an enemy."

The following soldiers from the 2-127th received the Purple Heart award during this tour in Iraq.

Sergeant Patrick L. Boggess
Wounded by IED, July 22, 2006

Specialist Steven K. Campbell
Wounded by IED, April 30, 2006

Staff Sergeant Timothy R. Cox
Wounded by IED, April 17, 2006

Staff Sergeant Timothy A. Ehlers
Wounded by IED, August 6, 2006

Photograph contributed by a member of the 2-127th

Specialist Steven D. Fosheim
Wounded by IED, July 3, 2006

Photograph contributed by a member of the 2-127th

Specialist Matthew P. Guffy
Wounded by IED, September 28, 2005

Photograph contributed by a member of the 2-127th

Specialist Lance J. Huebner
Wounded by IED, October 12, 2005

Photograph contributed by a member of the 2-127th

Sergeant Luke M. Luther
Wounded by IED, January 30, 2006

Photograph contributed by a member of the 2-127th

Specialist Ruben Macias
Wounded by IED, March 9, 2006

Photograph contributed by a member of the 2-127th

Sergeant Paul D. Mahlik
Wounded by IED, October 12, 2005

Photograph contributed by a member of the 2-127th

Sergeant Mark M. Meunier
Wounded by IED, September 28, 2005

Photograph contributed by a member of the 2-127th

Specialist Andrew S. Neumeyer
Wounded by IED, January 30, 2006

Photograph contributed by a member of the 2-127th

Specialist Christopher Rasmussen
Wounded by IED, September 28, 2005
Wounded by IED, March 18, 2006
Twice awarded

Photograph contributed by a member of the 2-127th

Sergeant Kevin J. Roland
Wounded by IED, March 9, 2006

Photograph contributed by a member of the 2-127th

Specialist Jeremy S. Roskopf
Wounded by IED, September 26, 2005

Photograph contributed by a member of the 2-127th

Sergeant Edward Shropshire
Wounded by IED, April 17, 2006

Photograph contributed by a member of the 2-127th

Specialist Nelce C. Sluka
Wounded by IED, July 22, 2006

Photograph contributed by a member of the 2-127th

Specialist Terrance G. Spranger
Wounded by IED, July 22, 2006

Photograph contributed by a member of the 2-127th

Staff Sergeant Brent T. Stelzer
Wounded by IED, March 9, 2006

Photograph contributed by a member of the 2-127th

Sergeant Jeffrey A. Vorpahl
Wounded by IED, July 24, 2006

Joseph Streeter

Brigadier General Barr, commander of the 143rd TRANSCOM, salutes four soldiers who were the first responders to the IED that killed Andrew Wallace and Michael Wendling. Andrew Neumeyer, later seriously injured, is the soldier on the right.

Update Letter to Families
from Battalion Commander Lieutenant Colonel Todd Taves
October 5, 2005

Dear Gator Battalion Families,

I write to you as we mourn the loss of Sergeant Andrew Wallace and Specialist Michael Wendling, killed in combat in Iraq on September 26th as a result of a roadside bomb. It is difficult to find fitting words following this tragedy; however, I thought it important for you to know how your soldiers are doing.

While the deaths of our comrades in arms has affected all of us, the morale of our soldiers remains strong and we are committed to honoring their sacrifice by continuing to protect the vital supply convoys supporting Coalition Force operations. In the 45 days the Battalion has been on the ground in Kuwait, we have already logged more than a half a million miles on the highways and roads of Iraq. The Battalion has completed every task we have so far been assigned, the result of the hard work and perseverance of our soldiers.

As we knew even before arriving, our mission is one that is often dangerous and unpredictable. Nevertheless, our soldiers continue to perform their duties in an exemplary manner. Be assured that we diligently work to reduce the risks from roadside bombs and other threats. With the continuing turmoil in Iraq, it is not realistic to think our mission will become a safe one anytime soon, but we can and have taken all appropriate measures to mitigate as much of the risk as possible.

Now fully settled in, our living conditions at Camp Navistar, while austere, are good. We have been overwhelmed with support from the home front and appreciate your letters, e-mail and care packages. We have also received a significant response to our school supplies drive to support Iraqi children in the Safwan area and will be delivering these supplies in the very near future.

As we begin the month of October, the weather is moderating and becoming more pleasant. As odd as it may sound, daytime temperatures around 100° are quite tolerable and lows down into the 70s actually feel a bit chilly. Soon, our soldiers will also start to begin rotating home on 15 days of Rest and Recreation Leave. Between November and the middle of June of next year, all of our soldiers will be afforded the opportunity to take this leave and have already "signed up" for their desired leave timeframe.

As we have been told by many soldiers and family members within our Wisconsin Guard family that have already experienced a deployment, it is often more difficult for those left behind than it is for the soldiers serving. I truly believe this and want our family members to know that you are never far from our thoughts and that your care, support and concern is vital to our success here. In this difficult time, please keep your soldiers, and especially the Wallace and Wendling families, in your thoughts and prayers. Thank you for your continued support and God bless.

INTERVIEW
Specialist Andrew Neumeyer

Warfare of the sort conducted in Iraq is devastating psychologically as well as physically. As soldiers we never knew who was friend or enemy. Every object in or along the road was suspicious. Average Iraqis trying to be friendly always made you remember stories of cleverly disguised bombs and suicide bombers. But for all the looking, those who were attacked rarely saw their attackers or the hidden bombs. One of the few exceptions is Specialist Andrew Neumeyer. He saw the bomb that struck him, called its position out to his team, and began to take precautionary measures just as it exploded, severely wounding him.

Specialist Neumeyer offers an inspirational story to all those who have been wounded. He is full of life, hope, and the same hard-work attitude he took into the war.

How were you injured?

SPC Neumeyer: On a night mission, one hour south of Baghdad, I was in the turret of my Humvee as the gunner. I stood up to shine a light under an overpass to clear it. I saw an IED and called to my teammates in the Humvee. I tried to get down, and right then the IED went off. I remember there was blood everywhere and then I don't remember anything really clearly until I was back in Washington, D.C., and had to choose whether to try to keep my right eye or not. I remember a little, just vaguely, my teammates pulling me out of the Humvee.

What was the experience of being medevac'd like?

SPC Neumeyer: It was all a blur. About the only thing I recall is the wind from the helicopter coming in to land and my team leader, Sergeant Luke Luther, who was also wounded with shrapnel, talking to me. Then I was pretty sedated. I remember Sergeant Luther asking me if I was okay right after it happened and I said, "I can't see" and "I'm spitting blood."

What was the toughest time for you?

SPC Neumeyer: When I had to reteach myself to walk. With a major head injury a lot of your body shuts down to work on the injured part. Plus it was tough learning that I was mostly blind. I was 20/800 right away. With good therapy and a lot of work since then I'm back to 20/80. At 20/60 I'll be able to drive again, at least during the day. That's one of my goals.

Joseph Streeter

Prior to his injury, Specialist Neumeyer received an award from Brigadier General Barr recognizing his efforts in attempting to save Sergeant Wallace and Specialist Wendling.

Tell me a little about the rehabilitation process.

SPC Neumeyer: Facial reconstruction and brain surgery was done right in Iraq at the Army hospital in Balad. Then I spent three and a half weeks at Walter Reed Medical Center in Washington, D.C., where they conducted an initial evaluation, removed my eye, fitted me with a replacement eye, and started me on physical and occupational rehabilitation. After that I went to the Minneapolis VA Hospital, a place that is very good with traumatic brain injury rehabilitation. I spent four weeks there doing more physical and occupational rehab, speech therapy, and spending time out with people for the first time. For example, they took our group bowling. I could barely see the center pin but I did pretty good. My therapist beat me in the game but it was fun competing. Then I went to Hines VA Hospital in Chicago where I spent two months and six days. It's a blind rehabilitation center. They had the best, most specific training for me out of all the VA rehab. Some of the classes included woodshop, computers (they got me my own computer with magnification and voice programs), a GPS system to use when walking and riding my bike, a visual skills class on other hand-held magnification devices, a cooking class, even a camera to use when taking college classes that lets me zoom in so that I can see the professor better. Now I'm going back to school for a special degree hopefully to work for the National Institute for the Blind. I want to help them evaluate work sites for the blind.

CHAPTER 7

Quality of Life

Joseph Streeter

Despite the stress of missions, or perhaps because of it, we did have opportunities for fun and relaxation. This war, unlike any before it, brought modern amenities to the battlefield, helping provide some rest and quite a few small comforts in a long, bleak year away from family.

One amenity that wasn't exactly modern but proved its ageless worth were the services of our chaplain, Lieutenant Colonel Andrew Aquino. He held weekly worship services in several denominations and provided invaluable support to soldiers who were going through difficult times. Stress from combat, from changing situations at home, from just being away from home too long—we all felt it at one time or another during the mission, and it helped many of us to have a chaplain as a spiritual guide. The chaplain also served as a gauge for Lieutenant Colonel Taves, letting him know how soldiers were coping and helping him determine when to request additional stress-counseling services for the men. Those counselors arrived at Navistar a few times during our deployment, most notably during the days following the loss of our three soldiers.

After a few weeks we were accustomed to the heat, but it never was easy to take. We ran from air-conditioned tent to air-conditioned tent, and even with the air on during the day, when crews often had to sleep, temperatures in tents soared to the high 80s and low 90s. Drinking four or five bottles of water an hour was not uncommon. Our medics measured temperature on three scales: wet bulb (showing relative humidity, here at 78° F), dry bulb or standard temperature (here at 122° F), and black globe measuring solar radiation (here at 142° F)

Enjoying a quiet evening behind the living tents.

Nathan Olson

Photograph contributed by a member of the 2-127th

ABOVE:

Chaplain Aquino met and prayed with the Imam of the mosque adjacent to Camp Navistar.

RIGHT:

Not surprisingly, prayer forms a cornerstone of most missions. Lieutenant Colonel Aquino, our battalion chaplain, led services for multiple faiths every week in the Navistar chapel. Lieutenant Aquino also provided counseling for soldiers who experienced stress during war or trouble in relationships back home.

FAR RIGHT:

Chaplain Aquino leads Bible study during off-hours.

Photograph contributed by a member of the 2-127th

It would be a lie to say we never had any fun or that life was, for the most part, anything other than comfortable and well-ordered. Still, the days passed slowly. The mission's pace ebbed and flowed. During the busiest times crews rarely received a day off. During the down times, though, breaks between longer missions were not uncommon. We filled our off-time by playing video games, chatting or writing email home, and calling home on the phones in the Morale, Welfare, and Recreation (MWR) facility. We watched movies and worked out in the gym. And enough entertainment—concerts, organized sports, cultural excursions to Kuwait and Qatar—was planned to keep us from inventing too much of our own entertainment—always a danger when soldiers get bored between missions.

Photograph contributed by a member of the 2-127th

Joseph Streeter

Joseph Streeter

Bands, comedians, and even Green Bay radio and TV personality John Maino performed on the Dry Dock stage at Navistar. The Denver Bronco cheerleaders and the girls of the World Wrestling Federation showed up to sign autographs and express their appreciation for the sacrifices our soldiers were making. And quite of few of our soldiers took the stage themselves to accompany the performers.

Photograph contributed by a member of the 2-127th

LEFT:
The band Crash Dance performed on the Dry Dock stage at Navistar.

ABOVE:
They even allowed our own Specialist James Wagner to sing along.

BELOW LEFT:
John Maino from Green Bay radio station WIXX messes with Staff Sergeant Corey Rodewald at Navistar.

Joseph Streeter

Sports, both organized and impromptu, flourished. Companies challenged each other in flag football and softball on the hardscrabble back lots of camp. Guys played pickup basketball and volleyball in the evenings, even late into the night, but rarely in the full heat of the day.

Joseph Streeter

Joseph Streeter

Joseph Streeter

Nathan Olson

LEFT:
The closest we came to having a swimming pool at Navistar was in January when the camp flooded.

BELOW:
Three of the bigger bases (Anaconda, BIAP, and Arifjan) did have pools. Here our guys enjoy the pool at Anaconda, surrounded by blast barricades to prevent injury from the frequent mortar attacks. LSA Anaconda was nicknamed "Mortaritaville."

Joseph Streeter

Joseph Streeter

Joseph Streeter

ABOVE:
The gift shop at Camp Navistar.

ABOVE RIGHT:
The laundry facility.

RIGHT:
A soldier buys a cigar from a vendor at the "Hajji-mart" outside CSC Scania on the route to Baghdad.

At Camp Navistar, all the little things, like laundry and haircuts and food, were provided so that we could focus on our duties. In addition to the standard PX (base store), a number of what we affectionately called "Hajji-shops"— run by local merchants who were allowed on-base— provided various services around camp, including a gift shop, laundromat, and a tailor.

Joseph Streeter

Joseph Streeter

Joseph Streeter

LEFT:
Our tailor specialized in making patches—little unit tokens, embroidered gifts, even quasi-official-looking nametags.

ABOVE:
The Camp Navistar tailor.

Joseph Streeter

ABOVE:
The MWR library.

RIGHT:
In the MWR movie theater we could watch movies only a few months old. The best place to get the latest releases was from the local Iraqis (pirated versions!).

FAR RIGHT:
The popular Green Beans coffee shop.

Joseph Streeter

Joseph Streeter

The MWR facility housed our Internet terminals and phone lines and offered DVDs and music CDs for rent, plus a library of used paperback and hardcover books donated by soldiers and Family Readiness Groups over the years. Toward the end of our deployment the MWR tent added several video gaming stations and replaced the ratty old couches in the movie theater with luxurious, comfortable reclining seats. A pool table, ping-pong table, and dartboard provided many hours of recreation.

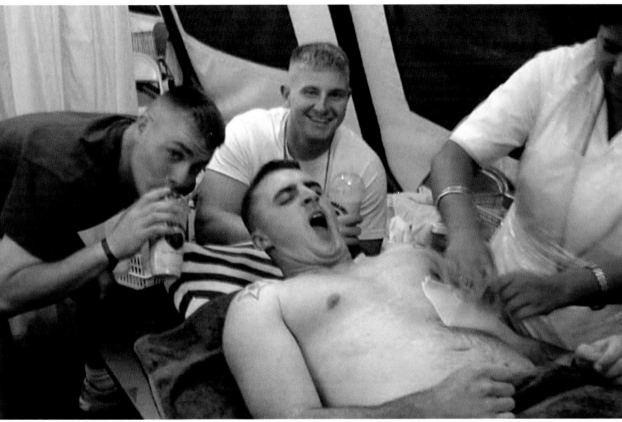

Photograph contributed by a member of the 2-127th

Joseph Streeter

ABOVE LEFT:

Sergeant Steven Fosheim gets "manscaped" while his buddies Sergeant Jake Paulson and Staff Sergeant Anthony Henner applaud.

ABOVE:

We had a very nice weight facility, named posthumously the SGT Andrew Wallace and SPC Michael Wendling Memorial Gym.

LEFT:

After a haircut the barbers gave a complimentary massage—not a western practice, but one we soon came to appreciate and enjoy.

Other facilities on-post included a state-of-the-art weight room, a barber shop where the contracted Indian barbers gave complimentary backrubs, and a coffee shop. When fast-food cravings struck, we had a Subway and a Pizza Inn—somewhat handicapped in its pizza production by the Islamic prohibition of pork products (no pepperoni!). We even had an occasional "spa day," with massages and "manscaping."

One of our soldiers, Staff Sergeant Scott Miesenhelder, set up a private Internet service that allowed soldiers to access the Internet from their tents. This was a huge a benefit well worth the $250 it cost those who subscribed.

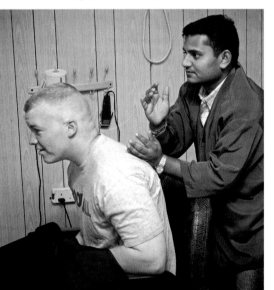

Joseph Streeter

Benjamin Buchholz

ABOVE:
Sergeant Jeffrey Stoleson helps himself to a big plate of fresh food.

RIGHT:
The ice cream man in the Camp Navistar mess hall was a friendly, familiar face to many of us.

FAR RIGHT:
Sergeant Terry Mulvey, one of our cooks, inspects a cooler of eggs in the kitchen area of the mess hall (the lemons apparently make the eggs easier to peel).

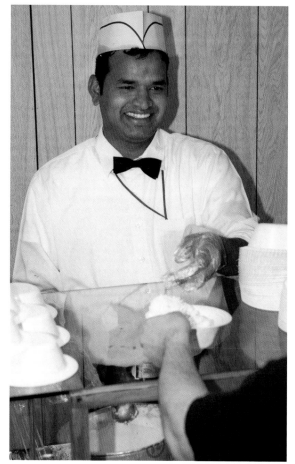

Joseph Streeter

Nathan Olson

Six hundred twenty soldiers need to eat, and Camp Navistar's mess hall accommodated them, along with other personnel on base. Our battalion provided seven cooks to help supervise a staff of contracted labor who prepared and served the meals.

Food at Navistar was excellent, among the best anywhere in Iraq or Kuwait. Served cafeteria-style, the main line always offered several choices of entree. A short-order line provided burgers, hot dogs, buffalo chicken wings, and other goodies. Fresh fruit and vegetables were available at every meal. And there was an ice cream buffet. If only our forefathers, fighting in the trenches in World War I or stuck in the jungles of Vietnam, could have eaten this well!

Of course, nothing could taste as good as a home-cooked meal, and nearly all of our soldiers got to visit home on mid-tour leave during our deployment. A few opted not to take leave, and a few met family or friends in other locations for their two weeks off. We found out the dates for our leave within a few weeks after reaching Kuwait and anticipated those coming days with as much fervor as

My son Jack (age three) screams in surprise as his brother Wesley (age five) buries his head behind me during our belated Christmas celebration.

Angela Buchholz

we did the end of the mission. In fact, being nearer at hand, it was the first milestone many of us began to count down toward. Because the battalion couldn't send all soldiers on leave at the same time and still perform its mission, our command staggered leave time across about nine months, from October 2005 through June 2006. When you got your leave was the luck of the draw, although each company handled the draw differently and sometimes could take into account special occasions like graduations, weddings, and anniversaries.

My leave happened in the dead of winter, in part because my sister was getting married on New Year's Eve. After a tediously long but joyous flight on a chartered commercial jet packed with other soldiers also taking leave (we'd been rained on during the customs inspection and slept overnight on pinewood benches in the military airport in Kuwait), my wife picked me up in Madison on the night of December 26 and drove us to my in-laws'. As Angie went in the front, I ran around to the back door and jingled some bells before stepping in to surprise the boys. I was mauled for a full ten minutes.

The two weeks at home went slowly at first, but toward the end of my leave the time just seemed to have flown. As my younger son, Jack, sat on my lap the night before I headed back to Kuwait, he put both his hands on my face and said, "Just let me feel you for a moment, Dad." It was more diffi-cult going back to Iraq than it had been leaving the first time. I still faced six long months, months that would turn out to be the most dangerous of our deployment. And unlike at the first parting, when my young ones had no real concept of how long I would be gone, this time my boys really knew what it meant when we said goodbye.

ABOVE:

Specialist Logan Fuller and Sergeant Zachary Zuehlsdorf dress up as Superman and a New York City cop for Halloween.

ABOVE RIGHT:

Specialist Asher Torbeck, Staff Sergeant Tim Cox, Sergeant Edward Shropshire, Staff Sergeant Tim Allen, Specialist Justin Roberts, Sergeant Joseph Trapp, Specialist Andrew Knaack, and Sergeant Michael Hoffman demonstrate the Christmas spirit outside the HHC Tactical Operations Center.

Even worse than leaving home again were the first three days back at Camp Navistar. It took that much time to get back into a rhythm, to forget the taste of home-cooked food, the feeling of sleeping next to my wife at night. The down time felt even lonelier than before, and the ticking clock that had counted the days until I could go home on leave was reset for another six months.

Down time like this was either feast or famine—either we were very busy or there was nothing to do. Impromptu and formal events helped this somewhat. For holidays, the mess hall did a splendid job preparing traditional American feast foods—turkeys, hams, pies, decorated cakes, and carved fruit displays. And our guys livened things up further, dressing up for Halloween and putting together Christmas decorations. We decorated each TOC with cards and ornaments made by school kids in our local communities, and each company added its own touches with lights, trees, and even an inflatable Grinch roped securely on C Company's roof to withstand the sandstorm winds. Packages from home, especially Girl Scout cookies, nearly overwhelmed our mail handling capacity. And guys picked up trinkets and interesting cultural items from bazaars in Iraq and Kuwait to send home as gifts. Traditional dishdasha robes, Arab headgear, prayer beads, vases, perfume oils, carved animals, and jewelry were among the favorite purchases.

Official opportunities to break up the monotony came via a three-day pass to Qatar and, for some, a trip to Kuwait City. In Qatar guys could take tours, fish from a traditional dhow, hang out on a beach, play water sports, and even drink an allowance of three beers per person per day (the rest of the time we were alcohol free). Destinations in Kuwait City included the Kuwait Museum, the Kuwait Liberation Towers, and dockyards dotted with historic fishing boats.

Photograph contributed by a member of the 2-127th

Photograph contributed by a
member of the 2-127th

LEFT: A beach in Kuwait City along the Arabian Sea, seen from the observation platform in the Liberation Towers.

ABOVE: The Liberation Towers in Kuwait City were built to commemorate the U.S. liberation of Kuwait from Saddam during Operation Desert Storm.

CENTER LEFT: A traditional Kuwaiti fishing boat moored outside the Kuwait Museum.

LEFT: Sergeant Bob "Doc" Schultz and Staff Sergeant Jason Janecek shop at a market during a cultural tour in Doha, Qatar.

Photograph contributed by a member of the 2-127th

Joseph Streeter

Joseph Streeter

LEFT: Falconry is a very popular activity for the locals in Qatar. Patrons could purchase falcons at this shop in Doha.

Private First Class Troy Newton and Specialist Eric Stilp visit the Ziggurat of Ur during a mission in Iraq. The Ziggurat of Ur is located at Talil Air Base, a U.S. facility. Convoys stopping at this base had the opportunity to tour the ruins with an Iraqi guide.

Joseph Streeter

Kuwait and Qatar are both friendly, westernized countries, and Kuwait preserves much of its Bedouin heritage. These countries have done a good job of spreading throughout their populations the tremendous wealth brought in by natural resources. Kuwaitis drive Jaguars, Alfa Romeos, Lambourghinis. But they wear traditional dishdashas, do not drink alcohol, and observe a very pious life. Any soldiers who visited Kuwait City or Qatar participated in cultural awareness training so as not to accidentally offend someone there. On our trips the highlight for many of the guys was looking out the window and spotting cars or taking pictures of the mansions that line the Arabian Sea. The contrast with Iraq—an oil-rich country that suffered under dictatorship and U.S. embargoes for many years—was stark. We often joked among ourselves that the surest way to end the insurgency in Iraq would be to give the average Iraqi a tour of Kuwait: "This is what you could have!"

During our deployment we grew through camaraderie and shared suffering, but we also brought a wider viewpoint home with us, thanks to exposure to Iraqi and Kuwaiti culture. For me, voting in the most recent election was especially important: the government institutions that keep us safe, clean, healthy, educated, and free mean more to me now than before.

Update Letter to Families
from Battalion Commander Lieutenant Colonel Todd Taves
December 18, 2005

Dear Gator Battalion Families,

As I write to you today, we have reached the 120-day mark of our deployment in Kuwait and Iraq. This means we have now completed one-third of our mission. During our first four months here, the Battalion has conducted 1,900 convoy missions, accumulating 1.8 million miles of travel on the highways and roads of Iraq. We have been extraordinarily busy, particularly so in the past two weeks. Most of the Gator Battalion is spread throughout Iraq on convoy missions as we approach the Christmas holiday. We expect that the next several weeks will be the busiest we will experience during our deployment here.

While Christmas here certainly seems much different than it would at home, there are still signs of the holiday spirit everywhere, including strings of lights, miniature trees, and even a large lit-up inflatable snowman adorning one of the company command posts. The flood of mail coinciding with the holidays has also been overwhelming. Thank you to all the individuals and groups that have sent packages, cards, and other items.

One thing I cannot emphasize enough is the absolutely tremendous job your soldiers are doing here. The professionalism, courage, and dedication with which they conduct themselves daily is remarkable, and you can all be very proud of them. Despite what you may hear or read about at home, we continue to make a difference every day, and the number of good news stories and indications of progress far outnumber the bad news.

Happy Holidays from all of us here in Kuwait. I know I speak for everyone when I say that we are already looking forward to next year when we can be reunited with our friends and families and enjoy the holidays together.

Benjamin Buchholz

ABOVE:
Specialist Lederhaus's
locker, padlocked
with his personally
monogrammed "Hoss."

RIGHT:

Lederhaus, the armorer
for Headquarters and
Headquarters Company
(HHC), is responsible for
repairing weapons. Here
he test-fires a .50cal he
repaired.

INTERVIEW
Specialist Daniel Lederhaus

While the majority of us spent our free time reading, playing video games, or watching movies, some put that time to better purpose. The Army offers soldiers a lot of opportunities for self-improvement: online coursework, colleges with remote branches that teach on bases, even GED programs.

Specialist Daniel "Hoss" Lederhaus was one member of the 2-127th who took advantage of these benefits. During our deployment, Hoss studied for and tested to earn his GED. It was hard work going back to school after fourteen years. His supervisor, Staff Sergeant Thomas Schuh, helped him study several hours a night.

But, oh, what a reward! The degree will help Specialist Hoss in his civilian careers as a volunteer firefighter in Fremont and as a hydroblaster with MidValley Industrial Services in Dale. And it will help him in his career with the National Guard. After fourteen years of enlisted time, he can finally be promoted to sergeant.

Tell me about your family.

SPC Lederhaus: There's my wife, Mae, daughter, Savanah, who is nine, and son, Dylan, who is three. Debbie, my mom, lives in Neenah, and my dad, Dan Sr., lives in Eagle River. They are divorced, but I'm close to both of them still. We do simple things together, snuggle, watch movies (*Shrek* and *Finding Nemo* are, or were, the current favorites before I left to come here), visiting

Photograph contributed by a member of the 2-127th

grandparents Earl and Marie in Waupaca, having campfires.

What do you miss about home?

SPC Lederhaus: Driving my '93 Dodge Dakota and once in a while just being able to spontaneously go somewhere—pack up the kids and say, "Let's go to Eagle River." My son loves Bruce the shark from *Finding Nemo*. I miss that, silly as it seems.

Benjamin Buchholz

How has your perception of home changed since coming here?

SPC Lederhaus: Home smelled different on leave. It was January when I went home for leave but the snow was melting, mid-40s, and everything smelled really fresh. It smells bad here most of the time.

How do you like living communally in the tents?

SPC Lederhaus: It's not so bad. After fourteen years in the National Guard, going to annual training, I'm used to living in a big open bay with other guys, so this is more private than that. Though the other day when the sandstorm came through I thought our tent was going to fall down.

Any funny stories?

SPC Lederhaus: We play cards at night, Staff Sergeant Schuh, Staff Sergeant Leslie, Specialist Wagner, Sergeant Roltgen, Staff Sergeant Althoff, Sergeant First Class Orlowski, and I. Those are the guys in my tent. And depending on what the mess hall served that day we might have to kick one or more of us out for the smell. Staff Sergeant Leslie is the chaplain's assistant, so we try to watch our cussing a little. Every two or three weeks we have haircutting day and it's like girls gabbing at a beauty salon, all of us lined up while we buzz each other.

Benjamin Buchholz

*Specialist Burger goofs
around.*

INTERVIEW
Specialist Ryan Boll and
Specialist Chris Burger

*While for most of our soldiers this
deployment was a transformative
experience, a few just refused to
grow up. Others seemed to have
brought none of these frat-boy
habits with them in the first place.
Both types offered their particular
specialty to their friends and teammates when confronted with
adversity and pressure: one type
teaching cleanliness and good
manners; the other demonstrating
that sometimes the most childlike
devices were really the things that
helped life remain stable and
centered.*

*Specialist Ryan Boll and
Specialist Chris Burger exemplified
these two ends of the spectrum
better than most. Boll is an admit-
ted neat freak who often found
himself cleaning up after his tentmates. And Burger, well, he's just*

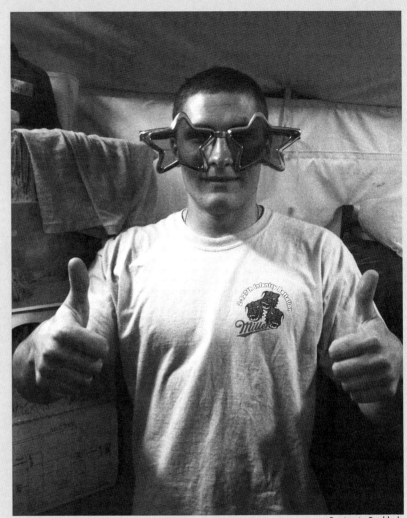

Benjamin Buchholz

*Burger. He was one of the unlucky soldiers who broke up with his girlfriend while deployed. He said he doesn't mind
too much, though—he's young and has a lot of party left in him.*

What do you miss about home?

SPC Boll: Waking up next to my fiancée, Jill, the weather, cooler weather, the not-so-dusty
weather. Just driving around, just being able to cruise around without Kevlar and IBA [interceptor
body armor] on.

Benjamin Buchholz

Benjamin Buchholz

LEFT:
Specialist Boll in his very well-maintained bunk area.

ABOVE:
Boll and his fiancée, Jill.

SPC Burger: I miss having a bathroom right in my living area instead of a couple hundred feet away. I miss being able to walk to the bathroom naked. I miss my backyard, trees, greenery, vegetation. Sand and barren desert gets depressing after a while.

How has your perception of home changed since coming here?

SPC Boll: I was in the Boy Scouts, so this isn't my first time away from home. But now, coming back on leave, I appreciated the freedom of being able to do what I wanted to do more. I hope that changes how I do things back home. When things get bad at home I'll think back about this place and think it could be a lot worse.

SPC Burger: My brother is married now, and my other brother is in a serious relationship. This makes me feel older. They're supposed to be my playmates, and now after coming back from here

Benjamin Buchholz

Benjamin Buchholz

ABOVE:
Specialist Burger made a shot glass from a spent MK-19 casing.

ABOVE RIGHT:
Burger mounted this photograph of his backyard on a sheet of plywood to remind himself of being outside in the snow. It hung beside his bunk where he could see it when he rolled over.

RIGHT:
Goofing around seems somewhat hereditary for Burger, seen here in photos with relatives at a family wedding.

and a little goofing around!

Benjamin Buchholz

everything is changed. I'll be going to school right away at Stevens Point. I'll be in a hurry to find an apartment. I want to have an actual home with space to myself where I won't be surrounded all the time.

How do you like living communally in the tents?

SPC Boll: It's interesting to see how I am as far as cleanliness goes, compared to other people. Jill has always told me I'm a neat freak. Sometimes I even catch myself cleaning up the other guys' areas.

SPC Burger: I'm used to it after basic training. Everyone is different so it is hard to accommodate different lifestyles. Some stay up late. There are loud TVs. Battles over the volume. There are hygiene problems in some tents but not in ours. Zinsmaster in our tent talks in his sleep: "Where are we going? Burger, where are we going?" he says. And then he'll go back to sleep and not remember it the next day.

Benjamin Buchholz

Boll's patriotic and drum-tight bed, one of only a few regularly made beds at Camp Navistar.

Joseph Streeter

CHAPTER 8

Redeployment

The countdown to leaving Iraq began the moment we set foot at Camp Navistar.

One of the first things to greet us there—displayed on the monitors in the Tactical Operations Center of the unit we replaced, shimmering as a screensaver on computers in the Morale, Welfare, and Recreation facility, scribbled on the walls of the latrines—was the outgoing unit's countdown. They weren't gloating. They'd done their time. They'd watched the calendar days drift by, the slices of the pie chart wane until only a sliver remained.

We thought it would take forever to reach that same point. But we also knew that from the moment we reached Iraq our time had begun to tick. Department of the Army policy states: no more than 363 days on the ground. We were well aware that policy could change. But we had an end date. Families made plans. And as the mission got busy and the deployment's rigors became routine, the slowness of the passing days was replaced with a sense of "Wow, we're halfway already!" and "I never thought it would go so fast."

Touchdown at Volk Field in Camp Douglas, Wisconsin, to the cheers of our family and friends.

We didn't hesitate in the end to give, sell, or throw away the bulk of our accumulated comfort items.

Joseph Streeter

We tracked our homecoming with passion. Each milestone we passed exactly according to the original estimates, keeping our return home on schedule, despite the escalating conflict in Iraq. Other units were hit with extended tours of duty toward the end of our deployment, but we were lucky.

During our last month in Iraq, milestones piled one on top of the other: leadership from 1-121st Field Artillery Battalion arrived on June 1 for a few days to learn about our mission and living conditions at Navistar; their main body arrived for training on July 23. We started to move our soldiers out of Camp Navistar to Camp Virginia (farther south in Kuwait, nearer the airport) to make room for the 1-121st's crews. The last of our soldiers to leave finished training the 1-121st on August 14. We conducted the official Relief in Place/Transfer of Authority ceremony on August 15, and the planes carrying our troops left for home on August 17, 18, and 19.

Sergeant Tony Henner, Sergeant Wade Melichar, Sergeant Jake Paulson, and Sergeant Steven Fosheim nearly missed their plane home. On their last mission during the first week of August they got stuck at Taji, a base north of Baghdad. Their vehicle needed minor repairs, but they faced an indeterminate delay while waiting for spare parts. The trip back to Navistar was a seven-day journey, so they called back to our TOC to discuss the problem. We ended up flying them back to Kuwait on a military transport plane. The soldiers from the 1-121st on that mission took over from that point on, bringing the convoy safely home.

The homecoming process began far in advance of leaving Camp Navistar. We had to schedule transportation, conduct training for 1-121st, and begin briefings for our soldiers on what to expect when returning to family life.

We also had to pack all the gear we'd been issued and the many incidental items we'd acquired over the year—and we had to do it in August, when daytime temperatures were over 130 degrees. But we were prepared to do just about whatever it took to get ourselves and all of our gear home as quickly as possible. We spread our gear out on tarps while customs inspection teams from the U.S. Navy searched for items that would be illegal to ship home, including hazardous materials, cultural artifacts, foodstuff, seeds, weapons, and pornography. Not too much was found. (I was the only one in my group to have an item confiscated: a map on which I'd penciled in a few routes.)

We returned home on three separate flights, big commercial jets packed with just our troops. The battalion commander chose whom would fly home on which plane, organizing each flight by

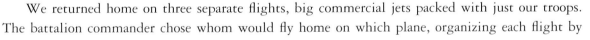

| I Got Here | 20 Aug 05 | I Leave Here | 19 Aug 06 | Total Days | 364.00 |

Total Time in The AOR
24.9%

Sentence Served
77.79	Weeks
544.55	Days
13,069.31	Hours
784,158.66	Minutes
47,049,519	Seconds

■ Sentence Served
■ Remaining Time

75.1%

Remaining Time
-25.79	Weeks
-180.55	Days
-4,333.31	Hours
-259,998.66	Minutes
-15,599,919	Seconds

Circle of Freedom

This chart appeared everywhere when we first arrived. (AOR=Area of Responsibility.) It was a depressing sight when we had counted down only a few days. Later it became a source of hope.

BELOW:
Sergeant First Class Joe Stevens helps one of his soldiers pack a duffel bag during the customs inspection.

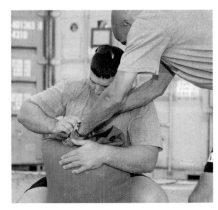
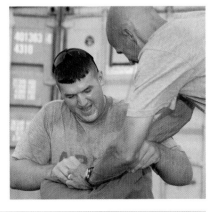

Photographs by Nathan Olson

Nathan Olson

The customs inspection teams conducted a very orderly, thorough, and blessedly quick inspection of the gear we shipped home.

company, with key leadership leaving on the last plane. It didn't matter much to us which plane we were on: they were all flying home, all within a matter of a few days. The planes stopped to refuel in various places, including Germany, Ireland, Iceland, and Hungary, seasoning our world travels. After each stop, when the wheels of the planes lifted off the runway the soldiers cheered.

While we were at war our families were without their husbands, but not without support. The volunteers in our Family Readiness Groups had helped care for families, provide them information about

Joseph Streeter

Joseph Streeter

Joseph Streeter

FAR LEFT:
A poster welcomes us to Liepzig, Germany.

LEFT:
For most of our returning troops, Bangor, Maine, was the first bit of American soil we reached. Here veterans gather in the airport to shake hands with our returning soldiers.

CENTER:
After the long flight, soldiers had to shave and clean up for the crowd expected at Volk Field.

BELOW:
The flight from Bangor to Volk Field took us right over our homes. Here Fond du Lac can be seen out the window.

Joseph Streeter

our deployment, organize family events, and just make life less lonely.

Working closely with the FRG was a small rear detachment of full-time personnel to train and take care of any soldiers from the 2-127th who went home early or who were chosen from soldiers outside our battalion to manage battalion business while we were deployed.

Stepping off the plane at Volk Field was an absolute whirlwind of emotion. A day anticipated for so long could hardly live up to its expectations. But it did.

We crammed our faces against the windows as we slowed on the

Photograph contributed by a member of the 2-127th

Photograph contributed by a member of the 2-127th

runway, our breath taken away by the greenery and by the enormous crowd—a thousand or more people gathered on the edge of the tarmac, all with signs, yellow ribbons pinned on lapels, baskets of homemade food, kids hoisted on shoulders.

As we descended the ramp, crews of soldiers lined up by the 32nd Brigade took our weapons and gear. We formed up one last time, shaking hands with generals and VIPs but looking beyond them, into the crowd. Standing on the grass at the side of the runway, I reached down and plucked a handful, amazed at how moist and lush it was. Then, released in orderly fashion by rows, we walked down a long cordon into the crowd, searching for faces.

I saw my brother first. At 6'5" and with my six-year-old son on his shoulders, he stood out from the crowd. I saw my mom, my wife, and my father, ready with a good handshake. We stopped to hug in the middle of

The battalion colors descend the steps of the last of the three planes that brought us back from Kuwait.

Photographs contributed by
members of the 2-127th

LEFT TO RIGHT:
*Debbie Taves watches
her husband, Lieutenant
Colonel Taves, wade
through the crowd
toward her.*

*Lori Fritz holds up a sign
up for her husband, First
Sergeant Steven Fritz,
and her son, Specialist
Jeremy Fritz.*

*Staff Sergeant Jason
Weisner embraces his
wife while his children
wait their turn.*

*Specialist Thomas Etzel
reunites with his
girlfriend.*

*Sergeant First Class
Clifford Williams poses in
his cavalry hat with his
wife, Renee.*

the flow of soldiers, right there in the cordon. Pressed from behind we moved on, under a tent for some shade. My children tackled me. They couldn't stop giggling. It was hard to tell stories: there was so much to say, but none of it seemed important. We were home.

The reunion was sweet but not permanent—at least not *immediately* permanent. We spent a few hours with our families, lounging at Volk Field, and then boarded busses to Fort McCoy for a few days of administrative and medical outprocessing. It was tedious but pleasant. Talk among the guys revolved around gossip from home, the amazing greenness of Wisconsin, the rain (we stood outside as it sprinkled one night), and strategies for completing the demobilization process most quickly. The process was organized into stations: military pay, medical, TRICARE (military insurance), Veterans Affairs, ID card, and military forms processing. We knew which stations in the process took the longest, when the lines were shortest, and how to fill out the paperwork most efficiently. Speculation about whether our command would let us go early turned out to be largely true: everyone was focused on getting home, the commanders included.

At last, fifteen months after we left for deployment, we called our wives or parents: "I'm done! Come pick me up!"

Most of our families had stayed in hotels around Fort McCoy, taking every opportunity between official events to see us. When we called it was only a matter of minutes before they arrived on base and we loaded our duffle bags into the backs of mini-vans and SUVs, rather than Humvees.

All the way home, from town to town—especially when we reached our hometowns—we were amazed at the show of support: banners, flags, hand-made signs. It was a beautiful sight.

Some towns held parades upon our arrival. Local VFW, Legion, Kiwanis, and other groups asked us to come to their events, to speak and share our stories. We were truly and wholly welcomed home.

Our reintegration into our families and communities continued after the parades, after the homecomings. Fortunately, there are many excellent programs in place to take care of soldiers returning from the battlefield. The Department of Veterans' Affairs offers soldiers counseling, medical care, even financial support, and most of our soldiers have used their local Veterans' Affairs offices for assistance of some kind. Others have enrolled as veterans in order to take advantage of services later in life.

The Wisconsin National Guard schedules events throughout the year to ensure that soldiers con-

Joseph Streeter

Joseph Streeter

tinue to reintegrate successfully. Some gatherings are mandatory Army training, and others are optional programs, such as marriage retreats offered by the chaplains. Our Family Readiness Groups also continue to be very active, finding good deals on vacations and family-friendly events for veterans.

An organization called Employer Support of the Guard and Reserve worked with our employers while we were overseas. This agency recognizes companies that do a good job of supporting soldiers and serves as a mediator if a soldier has a conflict with an employer while deployed or upon returning. By law, soldiers are allowed a "cool-down period" and do not have to return to work immediately upon arriving home. Some extend that period by taking vacation. And others take this time of transition to change careers or go back to school. But generally, a month or two after we returned, everyone had made the first steps back into their civilian careers.

It's not easy returning to a relationship after a long absence, whether it's a relationship with an employer or a spouse. One thing that helps, though, is returning to the military's routines. After three months at home we returned to normal National Guard schedules: a drill once a month, perhaps a meeting between drills, and two weeks of annual training in the summer. Now these drills seem like their own kind of reunion.

Our deployment to Iraq had been a long and difficult year, a year in which young soldiers and older soldiers alike grew in unexpected ways. And our families grew, too, some of them quite literally: babies were born, tots left in diapers eighteen months earlier were now reading, swimming, playing baseball. Wives and girlfriends greeted us at Volk Field with visible changes like new haircuts and new clothes but also with much more important transformations: new jobs and houses newly purchased in the months since we deployed.

The late summer and autumn of our return was a glorious honeymoon time—but not one without its difficulties. From past wars we've learned lessons on how to promote family reintegration and a soldier's successful return to the community. The National Guard in Wisconsin has provided us with many opportunities to learn, to take care of ourselves and our families, and to continue the process of individual growth that began in Iraq.

Joseph Streeter

Benjamin Buchholz

LEFT:
One of many storefront banners welcoming our returning troops.

ABOVE:
Staff Sergeant Jeffrey Gizewski dances at one of many homecoming parties hosted by communities throughout Wisconsin, this one at Appleton's Fox River Mall.

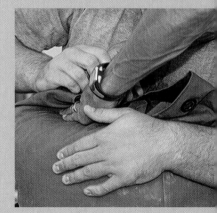

Update Letter to Families
from Battalion Commander Lieutenant Colonel Todd Taves
March 21, 2006

Dear Gator Battalion Families,

With seven months of the overseas portion of the deployment complete, I know many of you are now beginning to think about the Battalion's demobilization and eventual reunion with your loved ones. My purpose in writing is to address some redeployment related questions, but first I want to share with you some of the many accomplishments we have achieved as a team.

Since August of 2005, the Battalion has executed more than 3,300 combat missions while driving over 3.53 million miles on the highways and roads of Iraq. I consistently receive comments from the leaders of the units we escort on how professional our Soldiers are and the great job they have done keeping the convoys safe and rolling. All of this has been accomplished under austere and often adverse conditions. To date, over 180 of our Soldiers have been presented with the Combat Infantry Badge, Combat Action Badge, or Combat Medical Badge. These prestigious badges are earned by Soldiers that have been involved in IED or small arms fire attacks while on convoy missions. Prior to the current deployment of "Red Arrow" Brigade Soldiers to Iraq and Kuwait, the last time Red Arrow Soldiers wore combat patches and badges was following the Second World War. Each day our Soldiers are making new history and continuing the proud legacy of the Wisconsin National Guard and the Red Arrow Brigade. I could not be more proud of them, as I am sure you are as well.

On the home front, our Family Readiness Group program was recognized last month in a Pentagon awards ceremony as being the best in the Nation within the Army National Guard. This is a tremendous accomplishment, and I again offer my congratulations to our FRG volunteers, rear detachment personnel and everyone else who has worked hard to make our family support activities a success. Your efforts are every bit as vital to our missions as the work we do here.

Our accomplishments, however, have not come without cost. As you know, the Battalion has had several Soldiers wounded in the past few months, some seriously. Leadership at all levels continually works to mitigate the risk to our Soldiers, but Iraq nevertheless remains a dangerous place. Our Soldiers are truly making a great sacrifice by putting themselves in harm's way in the execution of our important mission. While every Soldier lost or wounded is a blow to us all, we remain committed to completing our mission with the same dedication and professionalism that has carried us through this far.

As to the matter of redeployment, I want to take this opportunity to also address a few rumors and questions I have become aware of so our families have the facts.

When will the Battalion redeploy from Kuwait? No exact date has been set, but we expect to begin leaving Kuwait in the latter half of August. While it is *possible* that we could be kept on active duty longer, I have no expectation that this will occur. Our replacement unit has already been identified, and all of our planning is currently based on the Battalion being in Kuwait for the full year. I have already heard the rumors that we are leaving in June, and others saying we won't leave until December. None of these have any basis in fact. We expect to serve the full year, no more and no less. If this changes, you will hear it from me, and any information to the contrary is not true.

Where will the Battalion redeploy to? Normally, a unit demobilizes through the same station that it mobilized at; Camp Shelby for the 2-127th. Last month we submitted a request to change the Battalion's demobilization station to Fort McCoy. The approval authority for this request is the 1st Army Commander, and we have not yet received a response. I *expect* our request to be approved since there are economies to the government in doing so, but we won't know for sure until we hear back from 1st Army. Once we know for sure where the Battalion will demobilize, everyone will be informed.

How long will demobilization take? Once Soldiers arrive back in the United States, most will spend about five days in the demobilization process. The number of units demobilizing at the time can affect this. It is important to understand that the Battalion will not demobilize en masse. As aircraft are available, Soldiers will be returned from

Kuwait to the demobilization station in groups. Some Soldiers may complete the demobilization process while others are still in transit back. Accordingly, this may not be a good time for group "welcome home" activities. The focus of the demobilization process is to ensure Soldiers transition smoothly from active duty back to reserve status with all of their personnel, medical and finance matters in order.

If the Battalion demobilizes at Fort McCoy, will we be able to see Soldiers during the demobilization process? As noted above, the focus of the demobilization process is to ensure soldiers are quickly and efficiently returned to reserve duty status. As such, families should not have the expectation that the demobilization period will be an opportunity to see their Soldier for any significant amount of time. We will endeavor to provide some opportunities for visits, but expect these to be limited, and Soldiers will be required to remain at Fort McCoy throughout the process, even if they live in the Fort McCoy area.

As we come closer to our actual demobilization date, more specific plans will be developed and published. In the meantime, I would ask for everyone's help in controlling any rumors you may hear. If you hear something you believe to be incorrect, or have specific questions, please pass them on to your FRG representative or our Rear Detachment personnel, who can contact the Forward element and obtain the correct information.

Thank you all for your continued support.

Update Letter to Families
from Battalion Commander Lieutenant Colonel Todd Taves
June 17, 2006

Dear Gator Battalion Families,

Today marks the completion of 10 months of overseas service for the Battalion. We are all anxious to complete our service here and look forward to returning home soon! For the moment, however, our focus remains on the mission at hand. Our FRGs and Rear Detachment personnel continue to be inundated with questions about redeployment dates and the process. I would ask everyone to continue to be patient. While we are continuing to plan for the redeployment, we will still be executing our convoy security mission for almost two more months. As such, the attentions of our leadership need to remain focused on our Soldiers here and keeping them as safe as possible in a dangerous environment.

Everything does, however, continue on track for our redeployment in mid-August. We have received redeployment orders to Fort McCoy and are already working closely with the unit that will be assuming our mission after we depart. We are in the process of coordinating the redeployment flights; however, due to OPSEC [operational security] considerations, flight information will not be released until shortly before the flights occur. This is also in consideration of the fact that flights are often delayed or rescheduled at the last moment. Next month we will provide information on how family members will be made aware of the specific date when their Soldier is expected to return. Confirmation of exact days will not likely be possible until about 24 hours prior to arrival at Volk Field, although we will be able to provide a general time frame for your planning purposes prior to that.

The basic redeployment plan remains as follows:

1. Soldiers will depart Kuwait and be flown to Volk Field. It will take several flights to return all of our Soldiers back to Wisconsin. These flights will not all arrive on the same day, and it is expected that it may take as many as 4 to 7 days to get all of our Soldiers back home.

2. We will allow for a brief reunion with family members upon arrival at Volk Field. Soldiers will then be bussed to Fort McCoy to begin the demobilization process. Soldiers will not be allowed to maintain possession of a personally owned vehicle during this process (i.e. don't plan to drop off a vehicle for your Soldier's use).

3. Demobilization should take 3–5 days, and Soldiers will complete the process and be released with the group they traveled with. This means that some Soldiers will finish the process and be released sooner than others who arrive on later flights.

4. Soldiers will be provided with transportation to their unit armory of origin, or may be picked up by their family members at Fort McCoy. Soldiers will be asked to make this choice before leaving Kuwait so that we can plan for transportation as required.

5. Further guidance will be published late in July as to plans for the Volk Field reunions, family contact with Soldiers while at Fort McCoy, and how families will be informed about specific flight details.

Thank you all for your continued support. Your Soldiers continue to do a superb job in the performance of a difficult mission, and we all look forward to our impending return and reunion!

Epilogue

I've struggled with how to sum up this experience of deployment, of going to war, of parting from one's family and returning changed. It is a massive life event for the soldiers and the families involved. It is a massive community event for the small towns that lost their policemen, their schoolteachers, their grocers, welders, attorneys, and businessmen for more than a year. Indeed, some were lost permanently.

Deployment wasn't a pleasure. That's not the right word. It was an adventure, for sure. And an honor, certainly—but is that expansive enough? Does the idea of honor include this concept of change, of coming home a different person than the one who left eighteen months earlier? I believe it does.

It was an honor to put into practice long years of training in the military profession and to lead and serve side by side with the best young men of our nation. It was an honor to serve the Iraqi people, although often frustrating due to the changing and difficult situation that country faces. It was an honor to come home to our families, to share our stories with them, to return to these communities accepted, even celebrated. And I feel honored that the experience lives on in me, as it does in the other thousands of soldiers who have gone to Iraq.

I've noticed a few things about home since I returned in August: the grass seems greener than it did before, the streets tidier; the trash is picked up on schedule; I don't worry about sending my children to school or about leaving my car or house unlocked at night; I pay my taxes with a little more pleasure than I did before.

When I have the chance to talk to young people about the military, I don't sugar-coat things. Iraq is dangerous. If they sign up for the military, they're almost certain to be deployed somewhere at some time. But if they do choose to serve, they'll come out of the experience changed, with a greater appreciation for service, for sacrifice, and for the little things at home that make the effort of fighting worthwhile.

Afterword

When Ben Buchholz sent me the manuscript of *Private Soldiers,* I was immediately impressed with his efforts to recognize the combat service of his Wisconsin Army National Guard unit, 2nd Battalion, 127th Infantry Regiment, 32nd Brigade Combat Team. Through his words and pictures and photographs by his fellow soldiers, the book records their year of conducting convoy escort and route security missions in Iraq. This outstanding unit became an integral and important part of the 37th Transportation Group, led by Colonel Michael MacNeil, and the 143rd Transportation Command, which I was privileged to command from July 2005 through June 2006.

The total strength of the U.S. military services is slightly fewer than three million men and women in the active and reserve components—less than one percent of our nation's population. There are nearly a half million Army soldiers in our active component with another half million in our United States Army Reserve and Army National Guard. Nearly three-fourths of these citizen-soldiers in the Guard and Reserve have been mobilized in the global war on terror. Among these few hundred thousand reserve patriots is the 2nd Battalion, 127th Infantry Regiment. Where do such citizens come from, and what motivates them to volunteer to serve and go into harm's way? These questions are answered here through the interviews and comments of the seasoned veterans of the 2-127th.

The 2-127th Infantry Battalion "hit the ground running," as we like to say in the Army. Their leadership, from Lieutenant Colonel Todd Taves and Command Sergeant Major Raphael Conde through their battalion staff and subordinate company commanders and first sergeants, was excellent. The battalion set the pace, leading 143rd Transportation Command/37th Transportation Group convoys in Iraq. The unit also demonstrated that it was the most outstanding battalion assigned to the 37th Transportation Group. Many times Colonel MacNeil tapped into the sharpened skills of these Wisconsin Army National Guard soldiers to improve other units within his command in maintenance, communications, and combat life-saver skills as well as convoy escort tactics, techniques and procedures. I personally traveled on fourteen 37th Transportation Group convoys. All but the first convoy were escorted by 2-127th Infantry Battalion guntruck crews. To a man, they were outstanding and extremely professional soldiers. I am fiercely proud of them and their strong Upper Midwest character, commitment, courage, and "can-do" attitude. These men are truly "salt of the earth" whom I would gladly go with into harm's way again.

Following the deaths of Sergeant Andrew Wallace and Specialist Michael Wendling on September 26, 2005, the entire 2-127th Infantry Battalion, except those on missions, attended the memorial service at Camp Navistar. The headquarters quadrangle was filled with chairs and benches for guest seating, and each subordinate company of the battalion stood in formation. There were few dry eyes as friends and fellow soldiers of the two fallen men read memorial tributes. I thought of my two teenage sons at home. I also thought, "Two killed, one seriously wounded, and this battalion is only two weeks into its mission. It could be a tough year."

I visited Camp Navistar at least forty times and became very familiar with the 2-127th. I was either getting a command briefing from Lieutenant Colonel Taves and his staff, visiting our Transportation Movement Control Teams or the U.S. Navy Customs inspectors at the border, coordinating with Kuwaiti border police and Customs officers on the movement of our convoys through their border crossing, or passing through on 37th Transportation Group convoys. I also attended several Sunday chapel services there, escorted my superiors on visits to the camp/border crossing area, flew with staff and other commanders to the camp for 2-127th Infantry Battalion–hosted professional development training events, and attended special ceremonies there.

I will never forget my last trip to Camp Navistar. I was there in early June 2006 with Brigadier General Keith Thurgood, my replacement, who took command of the 143rd Transportation Command in mid-June when my year of duty ended. We visited our subordinate units and met with our Kuwaiti border police and customs counterparts and then with the 2-127th. Following an update from Lieutenant Taves and the battalion staff, we went to the dining facility for lunch. While picking up a cookie at the dessert bar, I saw Sergeant Ryan Jopek in line and said, "Sergeant Jopek, I live in Nebraska and have a lot of neighbors with Czech names that end in 'ek.' Are you of Czech decent?" He replied, "Yes sir, I sure am," and he gave me a big grin. I thanked him for his service, wished him well, and bid him farewell. Two months later, back home on my farm in Nebraska after my demobilization, I was reading the "Casualties of War" page of the *Army Times* newspaper when I noticed Sergeant Jopek's picture. Below his photograph it read, "SGT Ryan Jopek, August 1, Camp Cedar, Iraq." I immediately throught of our chance encounter at Camp Navistar. I later learned from Brigadier General Thurgood that Sergeant Jopek had been killed on his last mission while doing the "left seat-right seat ride" with soliders from the 2-127th's replacement unit, a field artillery unit also from the Wisconsin Army National Guard.

This book is rightfully dedicated to Sergeant Ryan Jopek, Specialist Michael Wendling, and Sergeant Andrew Wallace, three young men who served their fellow man, the state of Wisconsin, and the United States of America with honor. In many ways, this book will answer the question when someday the grandchildren of the 2-127th soldiers ask, "Grandpa, what did you do in your war?"

—CHARLES J. BARR
Brigadier General
U.S. Army Reserve
Fellow Citizen-Soldier

Acknowledgments

I would like to thank my wife, foremost. She and all our families had the more difficult and less celebrated task of keeping a sense of normalcy in our family's lives during our deployment. My parents have been a great encouragement in my military career, and my grandfathers, both World War II veterans, were an inspiration. Lieutenant Colonel Taves and the staff and commanders in the 2-127th made many allowances during our deployment to permit us to capture the stories and photographs in this book, and without their support this project would not have been possible. Lastly, I'd like to thank the staff at the Wisconsin Historical Society Press, especially Kate Thompson. Her careful editing transformed this book from a high-quality yearbook with great photos into a living history with lasting value.—BB

I would like to thank all of my friends and family who supported me while I was away. And a very special thanks to my boys. You are the finest group of soldiers I have ever worked with, and I am honored to have been given the opportunity to serve with you.—JS

I would like to thank all of the leaders and soldiers of the 2-127th throughout my past sixteen years in the unit. The lessons I've learned while following and leading were priceless during our deployment. I would also like to thank my wife, who has endured not only my time away during the deployment but also all of the weekends I've been gone throughout my career in the Army National Guard.—NO

APPENDIX I

Mobilization Order

SUBJECT>SUBJ: DA MOBILIZATION ORDER 850-05 ONE/OEF/OIF

UNCLASSIFIED//FOR OFFICIAL USE ONLY.

SUBJECT: DA MOBILIZATION ORDER 850-05 ONE/OEF/OIF

1. REFERENCES:

    A. FORSCOM-3480 - OEF

    B. FORSCOM-3531 - OEF

    C. FORSCOM-3565 - OEF

    D. HQDA-2931 - OEF

    E. SECDEF MEMO 20 SEP 01, MOBILIZATION/DEMOBILIZATION PERSONNEL AND PAY POLICY FOR RESERVE COMPONENT MEMBERS ORDERED TO ACTIVE DUTY IN RESPONSE TO THE WORLD TRADE CENTER AND PENTAGON ATTACKS.

    F. SECDEF MSG 131954Z SEP 01, ATSD: PA/DPL, SUBJECT: PUBLIC AFFAIRS GUIDANCE (PAG) FOR PARTIAL MOBILIZATION OF THE RESERVE AND NATIONAL GUARD.

    G. DA MSG 101958Z JUN 04, SUBJECT: ARMY FY05 FINANCIAL MGT GUIDANCE IN SUPPORT OF CONTINGENCY OPERATIONS - CHANGE 1.

    H. DA MSG 220125Z JAN 03, SUBJECT: MODIFICATION OF ARMY ROTATION POLICY.

    I. DA MSG 052324Z SEP 03, SUBJECT: OIF ROTATION AND MOBILIZATION POLICY.

2. THE PRESIDENT, PURSUANT TO TITLE 10, USC, SECTION 12302 AND EXECUTIVE ORDER 13223 IN SUPPORT OF THE WORLD TRADE CENTER AND PENTAGON ATTACKS, AUTHORIZED THE MOBILIZATION OF UNITS AND INDIVIDUALS OF THE READY RESERVE.

3. THIS MESSAGE PROVIDES AUTHORIZATION TO ORDER THE RC UNIT(S) LISTED IN PARA 5 BELOW TO ACTIVE DUTY UNDER PARTIAL MOBILIZATION AUTHORITY (TITLE 10, USC 12302).

A. UNIT PERSONNEL ARE INVOLUNTARILY ORDERED TO ACTIVE DUTY IN THEIR CURRENT GRADES AND POSITIONS FOR AN INITIAL PERIOD OF UP TO 18 MONTHS (OR AS SPECIFIED BELOW) MOBILIZATION ABSENT AUTHORIZED EXTENSIONS OR REORDERS TO ACTIVE DUTY, UNDER THE PROVISIONS OF DOD DIRECTIVE 1235.10 OR SUPPLEMENTAL GUIDANCE.

B. PURSUANT TO PRESIDENTIAL EXECUTIVE ORDER 13223 OF 14 SEPTEMBER 2001, YOU ARE RELIEVED FROM YOUR PRESENT RESERVE COMPONENT STATUS AND ARE ORDERED TO REPORT FOR A PERIOD OF ACTIVE DUTY NOT TO EXCEED 25 DAYS FOR MOBILIZATION PROCESSING. PROCEED FROM YOUR PRESENT LOCATION IN SUFFICIENT TIME TO REPORT BY THE DATE SPECIFIED. IF UPON REPORTING FOR ACTIVE DUTY YOU FAIL TO MEET DEPLOYMENT MEDICAL STANDARDS (WHETHER BECAUSE OF A TEMPORARY OR PERMANENT MEDICAL CONDITION), THEN YOU MAY BE RELEASED FROM ACTIVE DUTY, RETURNED TO YOUR PRIOR RESERVE STATUS AND RETURNED TO YOUR HOME ADDRESS, SUBJECT TO A SUBSEQUENT ORDER TO ACTIVE DUTY UPON RESOLUTION OF THE DISQUALIFYING MEDICAL CONDITION. IF, UPON REPORTING FOR ACTIVE DUTY, YOU ARE FOUND TO SATISFY MEDICAL DEPLOYMENT STANDARDS, THEN YOU ARE FURTHER ORDERED TO ACTIVE DUTY FOR A PERIOD NOT TO EXCEED 545 DAYS (OR NOT TO EXCEED PERIOD SPECIFIED BELOW), SUCH PERIOD TO INCLUDE THE PERIOD (NOT TO EXCEED 25 DAYS) REQUIRED FOR MOBILIZATION PROCESSING.

C. UNLESS SPECIFICALLY STATED, THIS ORDER DOES NOT AUTHORIZE THE MOBILIZATION OF PROMOTABLE COLONELS OR GENERAL OFFICERS.

D. THE ARNG AND USARC WILL ENSURE THAT EVERY SOLDIER IN ANY UNIT IDENTIFIED ON THIS ORDER THAT IS MOBILIZED AND SENT TO A MOB STATION WILL HAVE TIME (PARTIAL MOB OR COMBINATION OF PARTIAL MOB AND COTTAD) REMAINING ON THEIR 24-MONTH MOB PERIOD TO ACCOMPLISH THE UNITS ASSIGNED MISSION.

4. MOBILIZATION STATIONS (MS) ARE SHOWN IN PARA 5. THE UNIT(S) WILL MOBILIZE AND MOVE TO ASSIGNED MS IAW TIME LINES ESTABLISHED IN THE FORSCOM MOBILIZATION AND DEPLOYMENT PLANNING SYSTEM (FORMDEPS) UNLESS OTHERWISE DIRECTED BY MACOM COMMANDER. UNIT STRENGTH WILL NOT EXCEED THE AUTHORIZED LEVEL STATED IN PARA 5.

5. THE FOLLOWING UNIT(S) IS/ARE HEREBY ORDERED TO ACTIVE FEDERAL DUTY UNDER TITLE 10 USC, SECTION 12302 EFFECTIVE:

A. MOBILIZATION DATE 13 MAY 05 AND MOBSAD 16 MAY 05

UIC DESCRIPTION COMPO PAX TOUR LENGTH HOME STA MOB STA

W8A9YB TNARNG ELE, JFHQ FWD11 2 1 445 NASHVILLE TN CP

SHELBY MS

B. MOBILIZATION DATE 06 JUN 05 AND MOBSAD 09 JUN 05

UIC DESCRIPTION COMPO PAX TOUR LENGTH HOME STA MOB STA

WNCQRK 203 MI BN MI BN TI DET 5 3 2 365 ABERDEEN PROV GND MD ABERDEEN PG MD WNCQR3 203 MI BN CO C MI TI EXPL 3 67 365 ABERDEEN PROV GND MD ABERDEEN PG MD

C. MOBILIZATION DATE 06 JUN 05 AND MOBSAD 09 JUN 05

UIC DESCRIPTION COMPO PAX TOUR LENGTH HOME STA MOB STA

WPLCAA 127 IN BN 2 2 0 545 APPLETON WI FT DIX NJ

WPLCA0 127 IN BN 2 CO A 2 182 545 APPLETON WI FT DIX NJ

WPLCB0 127 IN BN 02 CO B 2 182 545 APPLETON WI FT DIX NJ

WPLCC0 127 IN BN 02 CO C 2 182 545 APPLETON WI FT DIX NJ

WPLCT0 127 IN BN 02 HHC 2 73 545 APPLETON WI FT DIX NJ

APPENDIX II

Meritorious Unit Commendation, Approved May 17, 2007 *

SUBJECT: Meritorious Unit Commendation for 2d Battalion, 127th Infantry Regiment

1. The 2d Battalion, 127th Infantry served with distinction while engaged in combat operations during Operation Iraqi Freedom (OIF). The unit, a light infantry battalion of the Wisconsin Army National Guard's 32d Separate Infantry Brigade (Light), received its alert order on 6 May 2005 and reported for active federal service on 6 June 2005. The unit reported to Camp Shelby, Mississippi for post-mobilization training where it reorganized and trained as a motorized infantry unit. The Battalion arrived in Kuwait on 18 August 2005 and was assigned to the 37th Transportation Group. The Battalion formally assumed mission on 10 September 2005, relieving in place the 1st Battalion, 178th Field Artillery of the South Carolina National Guard.

2. The Battalion's principal mission was the escort and security of theater sustainment, deployment/redeployment and retrograde convoys executed by the 37th Transportation Group. Additionally, the Battalion conducted route security operations, route reconnaissance and provided security for vehicle recovery operations. The Battalion also provided maintenance and communications support for coalition forces, provided a Class I depot for units entering Iraq, and often escorted senior leaders on missions throughout Iraq.

3. The Battalion provided command and control for its four organic units; Headquarters and Headquarters Company, and Alpha, Bravo, and Charlie Companies with a collective assigned strength of 619 personnel. The Battalion also received as an attachment a composite gun truck company assembled from 100 Soldiers of the 111th Air Defense Artillery Brigade, New Mexico Army National Guard. This attachment was in effect from 26 November 2005 through 5 February 2006.

---

* The 2-127th's MUC award recommendation was filed before the completion of our duties. By the end of our mission, our troops had come into contact with the enemy 321 times, including 138 attacks by Improvised Explosive Devices (IEDs), 124 small arms attacks (automatic rifle fire), eight attacks by indirect fire, seven complex attacks (combination of IED, small arms, and/or mortars), and forty-four attempts to steal trucks from convoys. This recommendation was written and submitted prior to Sergeant Jopek's death; thus it mentions only the deaths of Sergeant Wallace and Specialist Wendling.

4. From 28 August 2005 through 19 May 2006, the Battalion executed 4,138 combat missions escorting convoys throughout Iraq, traveling over 4,497,505 total miles in the process. These missions often required travel through the most dangerous parts of the country, constantly exposing the Battalion's Soldiers to hostile attack. Convoys escorted by the Battalion were attacked 256 times during this period, including 104 attacks by Improvised Explosive Device (IED), 105 small arms fire attacks, 5 indirect fire attacks, 7 complex attacks and 35 hijacking attempts. Two Soldiers from Company C, 2d Battalion, 127th Infantry, SGT Andrew Wallace and SPC Michael Wendling, were killed in an IED attack in the vicinity of Shaibah, Iraq on 26 September 2005. Another 12 Soldiers from the Battalion were wounded in action as a result of IED attacks.

5. The Battalion's escort vehicles provided security for all major deployment and redeployment ground movements of OIF 05-07 including the 1st Infantry Division, 1st Cavalry Division, 3rd Infantry Division, 4th Infantry Division, 35th Infantry Division, 42nd Infantry Division, 101st Airborne Division, 1st Marine Expeditionary Force, 3rd Armored Cavalry Regiment, 11th Armored Cavalry Regiment, 172nd Stryker Brigade, 1-34th Brigade Combat Team, 48th Brigade Combat Team, 56th Brigade Combat Team, 116th Brigade Combat Team, and 3rd COSCOM. In execution of these moves, the Battalion's escort vehicles traveled to the following 43 coalition bases and facilities:

- Camp Bucca
- Northport
- Southport (Umm Qasr)
- Basrah
- Shiabah Logistical Base
- Tallil AB/LSA Adder
- CSC Cedar II
- FOB Smitty
- FOB Echo
- FOB Duke
- CSC Scania
- FOB Delta
- FOB Dogwood
- FOB Kalsu
- FOB Charlie
- BIAP
- FOB Cross Sabers
- The Green Zone
- Fallujah
- Taji
- FOB Warhorse
- FOB Caldwell
- FOB Falcon
- FOB Rustimayah
- FOB Loyalty
- Abu Ghraib
- Balad/LSA Anaconda
- FOB Brassfield Mora
- FOB Speicher
- FOB Summeral
- Remagen
- Taq Qadum
- Ramadi
- FOB Hit
- FOB Corregidor
- Al Asad AB
- FOB Warrior
- FOB Marez
- FOB Diamondback
- Q-West
- FOB Sykes
- FOB Honor
- FOB Iskandariyah

6. In conduct of its operations, the Battalion established an astonishing maintenance record which contributed directly to mission success. Inheriting a fleet of HMMWV gun trucks with a historical operational readiness (OR) rate of around 85%, the unit's organizational maintenance sections quickly set to work and within 60 days achieved a perfect 100% OR rate. Due to a strong leadership emphasis on both crew and organizational maintenance, the Battalion sustained an OR rate in excess of 98%. The Battalion maintenance team also planned and executed installation of numerous major vehicle upgrades to enhance capabilities and improve force protection for the Battalion's 153 gun truck fleet. These initiatives included installation of two different sets of add-on armor, installation of fire suppression systems, installation of improved seat belts and gunner restraints, the addition of an improved bumper system and fuel can racks, and the installation of various electronic countermeasures.

7. The Battalion's extraordinary OR rate maximized the number of gun trucks available to support the mission of the 37th Transportation Group. This was of critical importance during the high OPTEMPO "surge" period of deploying and redeploying units. During periods of peak convoy activity, the Battalion often had 95% of its gun trucks on mission for sustained periods of time. At the conclusion of nine months of operations, the Battalion had accumulated 513,867, or 12%, more escort miles than its predecessor unit had at the same point in their deployment. While this accomplishment was made possible due to the unit's outstanding maintenance program, it is also equally attributable to the spirit, drive and dedication of the Battalion's Soldiers who continually rose to meet every challenge that was presented.

8. Battalion communications section personnel contributed materially to the overall success of the operation and set the standard for use of secure FM communications with the 37th Transportation Group. Section personnel were often consulted as subject matter experts and called upon to assist other Group units. Completely dedicated to the Group mission, Battalion communications personnel made no distinction when it came to repairing vehicle communications systems; they were always eager and willing to help restore the communications capabilities of any unit within the Group in order to allow the mission to continue. The section was also instrumental early in the deployment in solving a significant communications challenge; an inability to communicate with the Battalion's route security elements beyond a range of 15 Km. To solve the problem, coordination was made with an adjacent unit for placement of a retransmission station on nearby high ground. This vastly extended the range of reliable FM communications from 15 Km to over 53 Km.

9. The Battalion deployed with a physician assistant and 18 combat medics that performed remarkably, elevating the standard of care for wounded Soldiers within the unit. Not content with the

standard issue individual and vehicle first aid kits, the Battalion's physician assistant ordered more capable tourniquets, bandages, clotting systems, and pharmaceuticals to create robust individual and vehicle life saving kits. The professional expertise and capability of the Battalion's medical personnel not only benefited their Soldiers, but all Soldiers of the 37th Transportation Group whose convoys they accompanied. The Battalion's combat medics and combat lifesavers responded to at least 41 casualty incidents involving U.S. Soldiers, coalition forces, or third country national truck drivers injured in IED attacks or vehicle accidents. Collectively, they provided immediate life-saving care to over 30 U.S. and Coalition Force Soldiers, and 18 third country national truck drivers. On several occasions, this care included performance of field surgical procedures and treatment of major trauma. Fully committed to providing the Battalion's Soldiers with the best chance for survival in the event of injury, the Battalion's medical personnel also implemented a comprehensive medical skills training program that resulted in 70% of assigned personnel obtaining and maintaining certification as Combat Lifesavers.

10. The awards presented to soldiers in 2d Battalion, 127th Infantry for their outstanding support of OIF are as follows: 24 Purple Hearts, 2 Soldiers' Medals, 31 Bronze Star Medals (3 with "V" device), 80 Meritorious Service Medals, 421 Army Commendation Medals (6 with "V" device), 265 Army Achievement Medals. Battalion Soldiers also earned 41 Combat Action Badges, 269 Combat Infantry Badges, 13 Combat Medic's Badges, and 547 Drivers' and Mechanics' Badges.

11. During this period there were no incidents of AWOL, 35 instances of non-judicial punishment, and one instance of conviction by court-martial.

12. The Battalion's exceptional performance in execution of all assigned tasks was essential to the overall mission success of the 37th Transportation Group, 143rd Transportation Command, and the 377th Theater Support Command. The performance of the Battalion's Officers, Non-Commissioned Officers and Soldiers was consistently superior, marking the unit's performance as exceptional as compared to other units performing the same or similar missions.

13. POC for this memorandum is the undersigned at DSN 318-430-7539.

—MICHAEL H. MacNEIL
COL, Transportation Corps
Commanding

APPENDIX III

2-127th Battle Roster

August 2005–August 2006

NAME	RANK AT TIME OF DEPLOYMENT	HOMETOWN
A Company		
Ackley, Darren James	Specialist	Wauwatosa, WI
Alcorta, Roger Jr.	Staff Sergeant	Green Bay, WI
Allen, Brandon James	Specialist	Wild Rose, WI
Allen, Steven Paul	Sergeant	Sparta, WI
Ammerman, Aaron Kyle	Specialist	Suring, WI
Anderson, Shane Patrick	Staff Sergeant	Holmen, WI
Anderson, Sten Christian	Sergeant	Oshkosh, WI
Arms, Scott Michael	Sergeant	Galesville, WI
Armstrong, Derek Wayne	Specialist	Onalaska, WI
Bahr, Dylan Joseph	Private First Class	West Salem, WI
Baltz, Richard Donald	Specialist	Chilton, WI
Bania, Kyle Andrew	Private First Class	New Berlin, WI
Barnett, Michael Christopher	Private First Class	Stevens Point, WI
Beach, Saul Oh	Private	Little Chute, WI
Bender, Jamie Dane	Staff Sergeant	Mauston, WI
Benrud, Joshua Jon	Sergeant	La Crosse, WI
Berndt, Christopher Michael	Sergeant	Merrill, WI
Berndt, Raymond John III	Specialist	Waupun, WI
Bissen, Roy David	Sergeant First Class	Black River Falls, WI
Bjortomt, Jake Kenneth	Private	Superior, WI
Blink, Donald Stewart	Sergeant	Tigerton, WI
Boenigk, Thomas Michael	Specialist	La Crosse, WI
Boll, Ryan Alan	Private First Class	Wausau, WI
Bortz, Adam Duane	Private First Class	Park Falls, WI
Brandt, Christopher Mark	Specialist	Menasha, WI
Braun, Erik Elton	Specialist	La Crescent, MN
Brehmer, Darell Kenneth	Specialist	Abrams, WI
Brueske, John Karl	Specialist	New Ulm, MN
Burclaw, Joseph Christopher	Sergeant	Wausau, WI
Burger, Christopher Peter	Specialist	Merrill, WI
Carlin, Brandon Joseph	Specialist	La Crosse, WI
Cieslicki, Andre Bruno	Lieutenant	Onalaska, WI
Clark, Matthew John	Specialist	Pelican Lake, WI

NAME	RANK AT TIME OF DEPLOYMENT	HOMETOWN
Clay, Richard Alan	First Sergeant	Antigo, WI
Clemins, Kyle Phillip	Sergeant	Menomonie, WI
Colgan, Shawn Michael	Private First Class	Onalaska, WI
Corbin, Joshua Cole	Sergeant	Madison, WI
Davis, Matthew Ryan	Sergeant	Rapid City, SD
Derington, Morgan M.	Private First Class	Moses Lake, WA
Derksen, Casey Tyler	Private	Waupun, WI
Devoy, Daniel Ralph	Sergeant	San Mateo, CA
Diedrich, Brian Thomas	Private First Class	Neenah, WI
Doan, Allen Benjamin	Specialist	Wausau, WI
Dornbrack, Corey Scott	Staff Sergeant	Merrill, WI
Duginski, Ryan Paul	Sergeant	Merrill, WI
Eckland, David Jonathan	Staff Sergeant	Bangor, WI
Ehlers, Timothy Alan	Staff Sergeant	Andover, MN
Eichmann, Jeremiah Hilbert	Private First Class	Fond du Lac, WI
Elder, Matthew John	Lieutenant	Barneveld, WI
Eldridge, Darrell Joseph	Staff Sergeant	Deerbrook, WI
Eldridge, William Thomas	Specialist	Marble Falls, TX
Ellenbecker, Dale Anthony	Captain	Mosinee, WI
Engebretson, Eugene Allen	Sergeant	Mazomanie, WI
Erdmann, Aaron James	Specialist	Dakota, MN
Fedie, Jamison Michael	Specialist	Jackson, WI
Felger, Richard Joel	Sergeant	Beloit, WI
Ferguson, David Harry	Specialist	Hartland, WI
Fisher, Franklin Joseph	Sergeant First Class	La Crosse, WI
Flanigan, Thomas Eugene	Staff Sergeant	Menomonie, WI
Forsythe, Derrick Lee	Private First Class	Prairie Du Chien, WI
Gano, Kenny William	Specialist	Gleason, WI
Garcia, Jeremy Juan	Specialist	Green Bay, WI
Geary, Gregory Arthur	Sergeant	La Crosse, WI
Getgen, Adam Brooks	Specialist	Wisconsin Dells, WI
Gilsongraap, Kylee Robert	Private First Class	Merrill, WI
Gray, Jacob Henry	Sergeant	Visalia, CA
Greeno, Ryan William	Staff Sergeant	Onalaska, WI

NAME	RANK AT TIME OF DEPLOYMENT	HOMETOWN	NAME	RANK AT TIME OF DEPLOYMENT	HOMETOWN
Guderski, Michael Thomas	Specialist	Ripon, WI	Krueger, Luke Walter	Private	Sparta, WI
Guderski, Mitchell Lyle	Specialist	Ripon, WI	Kuehlman, Timothy Joseph	Sergeant	Wausau, WI
Hackman, Roger Wayne	Sergeant	Holmen, WI	Lahvic, Corey Wayne	Private First Class	Neenah, WI
Hafner, Bradly John	Specialist	Holmen, WI	Lanzel, Michael John	Specialist	Holmen, WI
Hanes, Kristopher Alan	Specialist	Tomah, WI	Lato, Benjamin Peter	Staff Sergeant	Eau Claire, WI
Hanson, Isaac David	Specialist	Schofield, WI	Laureles, Jonathan	Specialist	Cleburne, TX
Hanson, Timothy Ardell	Sergeant	Arcadia, WI	Lauscher, Jason William	Specialist	Argonne, WI
Harper, Benjamin C.	Sergeant	Omaha, NE	Lehmann, Charles Robert	Specialist	Madison, WI
Harris, Jason Stanley	Staff Sergeant	Antigo, WI	Leitermann, Christopher Michael	Sergeant	Antigo, WI
Haun, Jeremiah Joseph	Specialist	Sparta, WI	Liss, Jason Paul	Sergeant	Plover, WI
Hecht, Ronald James	Private First Class	Cumberland, WI	Lubinski, Michael Kenneth	Specialist	Appleton, WI
Heise, Jay Douglas	Specialist	Fond du Lac, WI	Luther, Luke Mathew	Sergeant	Green Bay, WI
Hellen, Charles Benjamin	Private First Class	Beloit, WI	Maas, Cyle Joseph	Sergeant	Tempealeau, WI
Herbst, Jonathan Isenberg	Specialist	Eagle River, WI	Machler, Travis James	Staff Sergeant	Cadott, WI
Hermann, Timothy Andrew	Private First Class	Buffalo City, WI	Macias, Ruben	Specialist	Menasha, WI
Hernandez, Ryan Jon	Sergeant	Coon Valley, WI	McCormack, Terence	Sergeant	Marlton, NJ
Hersh, Thomas Allan	Private First Class	Homen, WI	Meyers, Mark Ervin	Sergeant	La Crosse, WI
Hodgson, Benjamin Jon	Sergeant	Mosinee, WI	Mildren, Derek Albert	Private First Class	Hurley, WI
Hong, Daniel Todd	Master Sergeant	Middleton, WI	Miller, Vincent Paul	Specialist	Sparta, WI
Hotaling, Joseph Scott	Sergeant	Niagra Falls, NY	Montgomery, Jeremie Michael	Private First Class	Monroe, WA
Inderdahl, Chance James	Specialist	Rosholt, WI	Muller, Mitchell Dean	Specialist	Hillsboro, WI
Jack, Robert William III	Private First Class	Lena, WI	Nelson, Stephen Jon	Specialist	Randolph, WI
Jacobs, James Joseph	Sergeant	Saint Paul, MN	Neumeyer, Andrew Scott	Specialist	Neenah, WI
Jerue, Marc Kendrick	Private First Class	Onalaska, WI	Neumeyer, Eric Frazier	Specialist	Neenah, WI
Johnson, Andrew Scott	Private First Class	Merrill, WI	Newkirk, Glenmore Michael Jr.	Sergeant First Class	Onalaska, WI
Johnson, Chad Michael	Sergeant	La Crosse, WI	Oleson, Charles David	Specialist	Friesland, WI
Johnstone, Kyle Edward	Specialist	Oak Creek, WI	Otto, Justin William	Specialist	Merrill, WI
Jopek, Ryan David	Specialist	Merrill, WI	Perry, Jon Wilburn	Sergeant	Milwaukee, WI
Joyce, Jame Chester	Sergeant	Sparta, WI	Petras, Jonathon David	Specialist	Bruce, WI
Juen, John Alan	Staff Sergeant	Evansville, WI	Pittman, Robert Wayne	Private First Class	Horicon, WI
Kane, Andrew Duane	Specialist	Irma, WI	Pregel, Ryan Keith	Lieutenant	Holmen, WI
Kanter, Harvey Walter	Sergeant First Class	Sparta, WI	Putzier, Jason Allen	Specialist	Winona, MN
Kelly, Brian Michael	Staff Sergeant	Onalaska, WI	Reiman, Jason Michael	Lieutenant	Plover, WI
Kielman, Jon Royal	Sergeant	Wausau, WI	Reinhart, Anthony James	Specialist	Onalaska, WI
Kirchner, Kevin Daniel	Sergeant	Wausau, WI	Rentmeester, Jason Paul	Sergeant	La Crosse, WI
Klozotsky, Ryan Paul	Specialist	Oconto, WI	Rice, Ryan Thomas	Sergeant	Appleton, WI
Knapmiller, Chad Lee	Specialist	Holmen, WI	Riedle, Vernon Leroy Sr.	Staff Sergeant	Appleton, WI
Kopec, Theodore Lee	Specialist	Arlington Heights, IL	Roberts, Dewuan Voshan	Specialist	Walnut, CA
Koszarek, Jeremy Michael	Specialist	Antigo, WI	Roland, Kevin Jack	Sergeant	Onalaska, WI
Krause, Duwayne Allen	Sergeant First Class	Junction, WI	Sanders, Corey Dane	Sergeant	Hillsboro, WI
Krogman, Edward Lee	Specialist	La Crosse, WI	Saringer, Steven Andrew	Private	Milwaukee, WI
Krone, Charles Mark	Specialist	Green Bay, WI	Sauter, Danial James	Specialist	Columbia Heights, MN

NAME	RANK AT TIME OF DEPLOYMENT	HOMETOWN
Schafer, Scott Dean	Sergeant First Class	Antigo, WI
Schimon, James Robert	Staff Sergeant	Medford, WI
Schmidt, Andrew John	Sergeant	Wisconsin Rapids, WI
Schneider, Robert Phillip Jr.	Specialist	Kenosha, WI
Schultz, Eric James	Private First Class	Oshkosh, WI
Simonis, Dean Maurice	Staff Sergeant	Wausau, WI
Simonis, Frank Ross	Private	Beaver Dam, WI
Smith, Nathan Patrick	Sergeant	La Crescent, MN
Smith, Reginald Julius	Sergeant	Wausau, WI
Snellings, Michael Joseph	Sergeant	La Crosse, WI
Steber, Kevin Donald	Specialist	Elcho, WI
Stelzer, Brent Thomas	Staff Sergeant	Cadott, WI
Stevens, Charles Rollin	Private First Class	Dakota, MN
Stoleson, Jeffrey Alan	Sergeant	Steuben, WI
Streicher, Daniel John	Private First Class	Onalaska, WI
Stuckert, Tommie Jim	Staff Sergeant	Antigo, WI
Swanson, Eric William	Sergeant	Marshfield, WI
Taylor, Donald Everett	Specialist	Eau Claire, WI
Taylor, Philip Stephen	Sergeant	Hortonville, WI
Thao, Steven Charlie	Specialist	Wausau, WI
Thies, Jeffrey Michael	Specialist	Round Lake Beach, IL
Thomma, Eric Marvin	Sergean	Fond du Lac, WI
Tibbit, Sylvester Jason	Specialist	Leesville, LA
Towner, Andrew John	Private	Onalaska, WI
Vandalsem, Nathaniel Cole	Specialist	Sparta, WI
Vansluytman, Elvis R.	Specialist	Brooklyn, NY
Verhulst, Martin John	Staff Sergeant	Onalaska, WI
Viner, Orrin Wayne	Lieutenant	West Salem, WI
Voelker, Brent William	Staff Sergeant	Westminster, MD
Walker, Brian David	Sergeant First Class	Eau Claire, WI
Ward, Gary Warren	Specialist	Brick, NJ
Warigi, Anthony Ndungu	Specialist	Neenah, WI
Wiesneski, Jeffrey Mark	Specialist	Merrill, WI
Werner, Dallas William	Private First Class	Holmen, WI
Whitehead, Dennis John	Specialist	Sparta, WI
Wilhelm, Scott Michael	Specialist	Stevens Point, WI
Williams, Clifford Dale	Sergeant First Class	Merrill, WI
Wilson, Thomas Lawrence	Specialist	La Crosse, WI
Wojtowicz, Travis John	Sergeant	West Salem, WI
Xiong, Tong Tou	Specialist	La Crosse, WI
Zimmerly, Donald Dean	Sergeant First Class	Baraboo, WI
Zinsmaster, Eric Michael	Private	New Richmond, WI

NAME	RANK AT TIME OF DEPLOYMENT	HOMETOWN
B Company		
Adelmeyer, Bryan Andrew	Sergeant	Oconto, WI
Aderman, Brion John	Captain	Milwaukee, WI
Anderson, Kyle Matthew	Lieutenant	Watertown, WI
Badillobeyer, Frank Michael	Specialist	Green Bay, WI
Bartels, Scott James	Staff Sergeant	Milwaukee, WI
Baudhuin, Philip Steven	Specialist	Sturgeon Bay, WI
Bay, Benjamin Brent	Specialist	Kaukauna, WI
Beach, Eric Jason	Sergeant First Class	Kaukauna, WI
Beard, Michael Joseph	Staff Sergeant	Green Bay, WI
Beaumia, Eric Phillip	Specialist	Madison, WI
Benson, William Jerome III	Lieutenant	Hartford, WI
Benz, Timmy Joe	Staff Sergeant	Green Bay, WI
Berben, Martin	Specialist	Gillett, WI
Berger, Duane Karl	Sergeant	Green Bay, WI
Bleck, James Lee Jr.	Sergeant	New London, WI
Boggess, Patrick Lee	Sergeant	New Auburn, WI
Boutott, James William	Specialist	Green Bay, WI
Buhrandt, Kurt Richard	Sergeant	Lena, WI
Butler, Rontaye Micquan	Sergeant	Milwaukee, WI
Callahan, Joseph Emmett	Sergeant First Class	De Pere, WI
Camacho, Anthony Sablan Jr.	Sergeant	Dunbar, WI
Cappaert, Craig John	Private First Class	Appleton, WI
Chaloupka, Mark Edward	Specialist	Two Rivers, WI
Charney, Beau Adam	Specialist	Green Bay, WI
Chavarria, Fernando Jose C.	Private First Class	Green Bay, WI
Cooper, Reece Edward	Specialist	Appleton, WI
Cournoyer, Kenneth James	Sergeant	Appleton, WI
Coveyou, Benjamin Daniel	Specialist	Porterfield, WI
Dallman, Andrew Gerald	Sergeant	Wausau, WI
Daves, Jesse Wayne	Specialist	New London, WI
Deisinger, Joshua Alan	Private First Class	White Lake, WI
Dozer, Daniel Wallace	Sergeant	Weston, WI
Duggan, John Wayne	Specialist	De Pere, WI
Dunst, David Brian	Staff Sergeant	Peshtigo, WI
Elie, James Robert	Staff Sergeant	Green Bay, WI
Etienne, Adam Tyler	Specialist	New Franken, WI
Fabbri, Steven Anthony	Specialist	Woodbury, NJ
Flegel, Scott Richard	Specialist	Green Bay, WI
Fredenburgh, John Edward	Private	Suring, WI
Fritz, Steven Dennis	First Sergeant	Oshkosh, WI
Gabrielson, Dane Robert	Private First Class	Black River Falls, WI

NAME	RANK AT TIME OF DEPLOYMENT	HOMETOWN	NAME	RANK AT TIME OF DEPLOYMENT	HOMETOWN
Garske, Jay Ezra	Private	Hudson, WI	Lease, Timothy John	Sergeant First Class	Verona, WI
Gerrits, Joseph Michael III	Sergeant First Class	Kimberly, WI	Letson, Andrew Christopher	Private First Class	Eau Claire, WI
Geyer, Scott Christopher	Specialist	Green Bay, WI	Lewis, Abraham Isaac	Sergeant	Iron Mountain, MI
Goodchild, Matthew Lee	Staff Sergeant	Two Rivers, WI	Litersky, Joshua Paul	Sergeant	Algoma, WI
Gordon, Darrel David	Sergeant	Peshtigo, WI	Loeffler, David Michael	Staff Sergeant	Twin Lakes, WI
Grimm, Adam Paul	Specialist	Kewaunee, WI	Loomis, Cory Allen	Specialist	Marinette, WI
Groll, Robert Edward	Specialist	Oconto, WI	Lundgren, David Timothy	Specialist	Richland Center, WI
Grych, Michael Mark	Private First Class	Oconto, WI	Mahlik, Paul David	Sergeant	New Franken, WI
Guffey, Matthew Paul	Specialist	Green Bay, WI	Maier, Mathew James	Sergeant	Fond du Lac, WI
Haines, Darrell Gerard	Specialist	Oconto, WI	Mashak, Benjamin Steven	Private	Winona, MN
Haines, Dwayne Gerard	Sergeant	Oconto, WI	Mattison, Kevin Roccio	Specialist	Webster, WI
Hammer, Scott Nicholas	Staff Sergeant	Greenville, WI	Matzke, Jeffrey Alan	Private	Green Bay, WI
Hansen, Curt Russell	Specialist	Greenleaf, WI	Merritt, Christopher Robert	Sergeant	Marinette, WI
Hanson, Jason Eugene	Staff Sergeant	Escanaba, MI	Merten, Miles Christopher	Specialist	Racine, WI
Hauge, Dustin James	Specialist	Neillsville, WI	Meunier, Mark Michael	Sergeant	Green Bay, WI
Hegner, James Aloysius	Private	Newlondon, WI	Micoley, Daniel Stuart	Specialist	Oconto Falls, WI
Hitt, Nicholas Daniel	Sergeant	Green Bay, WI	Miller, Joseph Allen	Specialist	Oconto Falls, WI
Hoefgen, Anthony Joseph	Staff Sergeant	Marinette, WI	Miller, Robert Richard	Private	Marinette, WI
Hollander, Michael Charles	Sergeant	Oconto, WI	Mommaerts, Joshua Steven	Specialist	Crivitz, WI
Hottenstine, David A. Sr.	Staff Sergeant	Pulaski, WI	Mosher, Jon Michael	Sergeant	Wausaukee, WI
Huebner, Lance James	Specialist	Prescott, WI	Moua, Doua Pao	Specialist	Green Bay, WI
Huelsbeck, Caleb Lee	Sergeant	Brillion, WI	Moyle, Kevin Patrick	Sergeant	De Pere, WI
Humphreys, Joel Jerome	Specialist	Oconto, WI	Mudrak, Jay Lawrence	Specialist	Racine, WI
Jacobson, Michael Douglas	Private First Class	Cushing, WI	Musil, Michael Paul	Sergeant First Class	Kewaunee, WI
Jarvey, John Clayton	Staff Sergeant	Green Bay, WI	Neckuty, David John II	Sergeant	Green Bay, WI
Johnson, Aaron John	Staff Sergeant	Menominee, MI	Nemecek, Dean Allen	Lieutenant	Green Bay, WI
Johnson, William Owen Jr.	Private First Class	Milwaukee, WI	Nickolai, Brandon Jeffrey	Private	Pulaski, WI
Jors, Zachary Marcus	Specialist	Kingsford, MI	Nygaard, Benjamin Mark	Sergeant	Duluth, MN
Kavanaugh, David Paul	Staff Sergeant	Kaukauna, WI	Nygaard, Jacob Carl	Private	Hampton, MN
Klemme, Anthony Charles	Lieutenant	Green Bay, WI	Olson, Adam Michael	Sergeant	Curtiss, WI
Knox, Alexander Frederick	Private First Class	Neenah, WI	Osborne, Dewitt Thomas	Specialist	Washington, DC
Knutson, Dustin Eckhart	Private First Class	Marinette, WI	Padgett, Timothy James	Staff Sergeant	Marinette, WI
Kocken, William Alan	Specialist	De Pere, WI	Paschke, Gerrard Orville	Specialist	Sturgeon Bay, WI
Koskelin, Nathan Daniel	Private First Class	Kaukauna, WI	Paschke, Nolan Mitchell	Specialist	Luxemburg, WI
Kostichka, Brian Charles	Staff Sergeant	Algoma, WI	Paul, Edwin Frederick III	Sergeant	Marinette, WI
Krajenka, Derrick Tyler	Private First Class	Milan, WI	Perkins, Joshua James	Sergeant	Neenah, WI
Kreutzberg, Andrew John II	Specialist	Clintonville, WI	Perkins, Josiah James	Private	Neenah, WI
Kuhrt, Brennan Mitchell	Private First Class	Rice Lake, WI	Pichette, Nicholas Michael	Specialist	Algoma, WI
Lang, Adam Thomas	Private	Marinette, WI	Piumbroeck, William Joseph	Specialist	Green Bay, WI
Lange, Andrew James	Specialist	Green Bay, WI	Prucha, John James	Specialist	Manitowoc, WI
Larsen, Jeffrey James	Staff Sergeant	Green Bay, WI	Quirk, Joseph Andrew	Specialist	Green Bay, WI
Leair, Aaron Francis	Specialist	Appleton, WI	Raab, Edward William	Sergeant	Oshkosh, WI

NAME	RANK AT TIME OF DEPLOYMENT	HOMETOWN
Rasmussen, Christopher Adam	Specialist	Green Bay, WI
Recka, William Joseph	Sergeant	New Franken, WI
Riley, Stuart Edward Jr.	Specialist	Seymoure, WI
Rine, Shawn William	Specialist	Elton, WI
Ritchie, Aaron Michael	Staff Sergeant	Hortonville, WI
Rivenes, Cody Joe	Specialist	Green Bay, WI
Rosenow, Arlyn Elmer Edwin	Sergeant	Pulaski, WI
Rosholt, Randy Peter	Specialist	Milwaukee, WI
Sattler, Steven Paul	Specialist	Maribel, WI
Schmitz, Brian Michael	Sergeant	Green Bay, WI
Schussler, Seth Andrew	Private First Class	Kaukauna, WI
Schussler, Tyler David	Specialist	Green Bay, WI
Scott, Billy Dean	Specialist	Menominee, MI
Scott, Fred Charles III	Private First Class	Beldenville, WI
Scott, Robert Richard	Specialist	Lakewood, NJ
Senstad, Jeremy Steven	Specialist	River Falls, WI
Shaffer, Kenneth Charles	Sergeant First Class	Ripon, WI
Sheehy, Anthony James	Private First Class	Reedsville, WI
Sluka, Nelce Charles	Private First Class	Dresser, WI
Smith, Brant Randall	Private	Unity, WI
Smith, Justin David	Specialist	Medford, WI
Smits, Jason John	Specialist	Suamico, WI
Snyder, Alexander Nicholas S.	Private First Class	Rice Lake, WI
Somers, David Oral Jr.	Specialist	Peshtigo, WI
Somers, Thomas Lynn	Sergeant	Marinette, WI
Sonnentag, Travis James	Private First Class	Cadott, WI
Sotka, James David	Sergeant	Peshtigo, WI
Spranger, Terrance Gene Jr.	Specialist	Crivitz, WI
Stamm, Gregory Patrick	Sergeant	Green Bay, WI
Stanke, Daniel Jerome	Specialist	Bonduel, WI
Stevens, Francis Joseph	Staff Sergeant	Green Bay, WI
Stumpf, Jeremy Michael	Specialist	Lena, WI
Tappen, Christopher Scott	Sergeant	De Pere, WI
Taylor, Eric Michael	Private	Green Bay, WI
Tenor, Eric Matthew	Specialist	Green Bay, WI
Tessmer, Donald Lee	Sergeant	Menominee, MI
Thao, Chia Chong	Private	De Pere, WI
Thiel, Jeffrey James	Sergeant	Little Chute, WI
Tilkens, Todd Michael	Sergeant First Class	Green Bay, WI
Tommarello, Michael John	Sergeant	De Pere, WI
Trindal, Michael James	Specialist	Niagara, WI
Turk, Andrew Inwoo	Sergeant	Oshkosh, WI

NAME	RANK AT TIME OF DEPLOYMENT	HOMETOWN
Vancuyk, Adam Joseph	Private First Class	Kimberly, WI
Vandehei Roland John Jr.	Specialist	Oneida, WI
Vandenplas Jacob John	Specialist	Abrams, WI
Vandyke, David Samuel	Sergeant	Green Bay, WI
Vanvonderen, Joseph Raymond	Sergeant	Green Bay, WI
Velure, Anthony Palmer	Private First Class	River Falls, WI
Verlezza, Michael Anthony	Private First Class	Oneida, WI
Verstegen, Timothy Francis	Specialist	Little Chute, WI
Vorpahl, Jeffrey Allen	Sergeant	Green Bay, WI
Vosnos, John Michael	Lieutenant	Barrington, IL
Waln, Max Anthony	Sergeant	Oshkosh, WI
Ward, Daniel Todd	Specialist	Oconto Falls, WI
Ward, Matthew Leland	Specialist	Oconto Falls, WI
Werner, Richard Paul	Sergeant First Class	Hancock, WI
Weyer, Duane Robert	Sergeant First Class	Mosinee, WI
Wieber, Jason James	Specialist	Green Bay, WI
Wilson, Jamie Jon	Specialist	Two Rivers, WI
Winkelman, Steven Larson	Private First Class	Dresser, WI
Yang, Blissful	Sergeant	Green Bay, WI
Ziegler, Scott Matthew	Specialist	Ripon, WI
Zubich, Kenneth	Sergeant	Appleton, WI

C Company

NAME	RANK AT TIME OF DEPLOYMENT	HOMETOWN
Abbs, Jerry Austin	Sergeant	Fontana, CA
Amend, Jeffrey Leo	Staff Sergeant	Ripon, WI
Arnold, Todd James	Sergeant	Appleton, WI
Arquette, Todd Allen	Sergeant	Green Bay, WI
Augsburger, Daniel Trent	Specialist	Oshkosh, WI
Beauprey, James Robert	Private First Class	Horicon, WI
Becker, Nathan Andrew	Specialist	Beaver Dam, WI
Bednarek, Brian Joseph	Sergeant	Fond du Lac, WI
Beirne, Jeffrey Alan	Specialist	Oakfield, WI
Belflower, Andrew Brian	Specialist	Chilton, WI
Boyd, Kevin Richard	Sergeant	Kenosha, WI
Bratz, Shane Alan	Sergeant	Kaukauna, WI
Bronkhorst, Gerald John Jr.	Specialist	Little Suamico, WI
Brown, Edward Lee	Specialist	Horicon, WI
Brown, Lars Martin	Lieutenant	Hortonville, WI
Brown, Nels Kristopher	Sergeant First Class	Oshkosh, WI
Bruesch, Cody Ryan	Specialist	Waupun, WI
Brunet, Nash Allen	Specialist	Fond du Lac, WI
Bucher, Bradley Thomas	Lieutenant	Green Bay, WI

NAME	RANK AT TIME OF DEPLOYMENT	HOMETOWN	NAME	RANK AT TIME OF DEPLOYMENT	HOMETOWN
Buss, Tyler Ray	Specialist	Horicon, WI	Higgins, Timothy Shawn Jr.	Private First Class	Fond du Lac, WI
Campbell, Steven Kenneth	Specialist	Milwaukee, WI	Hilgers, Robert Alfred Jr.	Specialist	Neenah, WI
Cerney, Jay Francis	Sergeant	Eldorado, WI	Hoeper, Ryan John	Sergeant	Neenah, WI
Christianson, David Ronald	First Sergeant	Oshkosh, WI	Horn, Steven Richard	Sergeant	Fond du Lac, WI
Cramer, Matthew James	Specialist	Appleton, WI	Huempfner, Joshua Robert	Private	Brandon, WI
Cutter, Kevin Joseph	Specialist	Fond du Lac, WI	Isbell, Patrick Lee	Private First Class	Kaukauna, WI
Danor, Stuart Chad	Sergeant	Fond du Lac, WI	Jakubovsky, Thomas James	Master Sergeant	Green Bay, WI
Dawson, Lucas Andrew	Specialist	Cambria, WI	Janecek, Jason Allen	Staff Sergeant	Ashland, WI
Debroux, Justin Michael	Specialist	Richfield, WI	Jarapko, David Andrew	Staff Sergeant	Oshkosh, WI
Degroff, Joshua Dean	Specialist	Beaver Dam, WI	Jarosinski, Christopher Jose	Staff Sergeant	Wisconsin Rapids, WI
Demaa, Derek Dean	Specialist	Brandon, WI	Jaworski, John Daniel	Sergeant	Fond du Lac, WI
Dickson, Scott David	Staff Sergeant	Cambridge, WI	Jaworski, Robert Douglas	Staff Sergeant	Fond du Lac, WI
Diederichs, Jeffrey Scott	Sergeant	Sheboygan, WI	Johnson, Curt Thomas	Sergeant	Oshkosh, WI
Dietzler, John Linden II	Sergeant First Class	Green Bay, WI	Johnson, Leroy Edward Jr.	Specialist	Fall Creek, WI
Dittmann, Jake Allen	Sergeant	Green Bay, WI	Johnson, William Anthony	Staff Sergeant	Fond du Lac, WI
Dombrowski, Stephen Lisle	Specialist	Green Lake, WI	Jome, Reid Erskine	Specialist	Neenah, WI
Dorn, Michael Philip	Private	Neenah, WI	Kaiser, Zachary John	Private	Mount Calvary, WI
Doro, Joshua James	Staff Sergeant	Princeton, WI	Kelm, Daniel William	Sergeant	Oshkosh, WI
Drake, Michael Jon	Sergeant First Class	Oshkosh, WI	Kempen, Vernon Charles	Sergeant	Waupun, WI
Ellis, Jerome Edwin	Sergeant	Muskego, WI	Keplin, Adam Lee	Sergeant	Fond du Lac, WI
Elsinger, James Allan	Specialist	Oak Creek, WI	Kerr, Timothy Clifford	Specialist	Loudonville, OH
Essick, Nicholas Robert	Specialist	Menomonie, WI	Kincheloe, Roscoe Lloyd	Sergeant	Menasha, WI
Etzel, Thomas Edward III	Private First Class	Stevens Point, WI	Koch, Jeffrey Ralph	Specialist	Oshkosh, WI
Fischer, Anthony Steven	Private First Class	New London, WI	Koopman, Patrick Steven	Specialist	Cochrane, WI
Fisher, Sean Shariff	Specialist	Mount Holly, NJ	Korhonen, Jason William	Specialist	Sheboygan, WI
Fosheim, Steven Douglas	Specialist	Whitewater, WI	Krivoshein, James Kenneth Jr.	Sergeant First Class	Greenville, WI
Foss, Donald Robert	Sergeant	Sarona, WI	Kronschnabel, Matthew Raymond	Sergeant First Class	Milwaukee, WI
Fritz, Jeremy	Private First Class	Oshkosh, WI	Krueger, Eric Paul	Lieutenant	Horicon, WI
Fuller, Logan Michael	Specialist	Oshkosh, WI	Kuen, Aaron Charles	Specialist	Horicon, WI
Garbe, Keith Michael	Staff Sergeant	Green Bay, WI	Lacrosse, Anthony	Sergeant	Portage, WI
Gassner, Jeffrey Allen	Specialist	Fond du Lac, WI	Larson, Andrew John	Specialist	Fond du Lac , WI
Gerrits, Tyler Richard	Staff Sergeant	Green Bay, WI	Lehrer, Matthew George	Sergeant First Class	Antigo, WI
Glamann, Michael Scot II	Specialist	Waupun, WI	Leitsch, James Elliott	Private First Class	Appleton, WI
Goodman, John Thomas	Specialist	Eau Claire, WI	Likens, Jonathan Ryan	Specialist	Loveland, OH
Grube, Jason Michael	Specialist	Chilton, WI	Luedke, Kyle Edwin	Staff Sergeant	Glendale, WI
Gubin, Jacob Lee	Private First Class	Fox Lake, WI	Mabee, Matthew Paul	Sergeant	West Allis, WI
Guilette, Christopher Glenn	Specialist	Appleton, WI	Magee, Albert Ray Jr.	Private First Class	Milwaukee, WI
Hagman, David Lyle	Specialist	N Fond du Lac, WI	Malone, Thomas John	Specialist	Waukesha, WI
Heckel, Aaron John	Private First Class	Marinette, WI	Malwitz, Adam John	Specialist	Fond du Lac, WI
Hedtke, Jesse Joe	Staff Sergeant	New London, WI	Mattice, Robert Ronald III	Specialist	Berlin, WI
Henner, Anthony Paul	Sergeant	Milwaukee, WI	McKeen, Jordan Robert	Private First Class	Chilton, WI
Hert, Christian Michael	Private First Class	Oshkosh, WI	Melichar, Wade Alan	Sergeant	Appleton, WI

NAME	RANK AT TIME OF DEPLOYMENT	HOMETOWN	NAME	RANK AT TIME OF DEPLOYMENT	HOMETOWN
Miley, James David II	Sergeant First Class	Lomira, WI	Schmidtquist, Justin Jay	Specialist	Horicon, WI
Montalvo, Nathan Alexander	Specialist	Appleton, WI	Schmuhl, Patrick Steven	Specialist	Fond du Lac, WI
Morris, Travis James	Sergeant	Shawano, WI	Schneidewend, Dean Alan	Specialist	Oshkosh, WI
Mulvey, Terry Lee	Sergeant	Oshkosh, WI	Schroeder, Charles Gordon	Specialist	Fond du Lac, WI
Nagel, Jared John	Lieutenant	Plover, WI	Schueler, James Steven	Specialist	Green Bay, WI
Newton, Troy Raymond	Specialist	Taycheedah, WI	Schultz, Robert James Jr.	Sergeant	Fond du Lac, WI
Nicchetta, Martin Joseph	Private First Class	Oshkosh, WI	Schumm, Edward Carlos	Sergeant	Paso Robles, CA
Nyman, Andrew Jacob	Private First Class	Black River Falls, WI	Scott, Jonathan D.	Sergeant	Alliance, OH
Oestreich, Ross Patrick	Specialist	Waupaca, WI	Simon, Jeffrey John	Specialist	Fond du Lac, WI
Olig, Todd Richard	Staff Sergeant	Brownsville, WI	Sorensen, Justin Edward	Specialist	Ripon, WI
Oliphant, Randy Lee	Staff Sergeant	Appleton, WI	Spatz, Paul David	Specialist	Wausau, WI
Oliphant, Ryan Curtis	Specialist	La Crosse, WI	Stephens, Robert Brett	Staff Sergeant	Madison, WI
Olson, Nathan Paul	Lieutenant	Columbus, WI	Stilp, Eric Jon	Specialist	Larsen, WI
O'Neill, Thomas McGuire	Private First Class	Waupaca, WI	Stogbauer, Matthew Robert	Sergeant	Van Dyne, WI
Pariseau, Steven John	Sergeant	Tomah, WI	Stonecipher, Scott William	Staff Sergeant	Kewaskum, WI
Paul, Jonathan Matthew	Sergeant	Fond du Lac, WI	Streeter, Joseph Arden	Staff Sergeant	Fond du Lac, WI
Paul, Jordan Michael	Specialist	Fond du Lac, WI	Strobush, Seth Michael	Private First Class	Winona , MN
Paulson, Jake Daniel	Sergeant	Waukesha, WI	Struebing, Dennis Leroy	Specialist	Plymouth, WI
Peper, Joshua Charles	Specialist	New Berlin, WI	Stuczynski, Timothy Frank	Specialist	Kaukauna, WI
Peterson, Erick James	Staff Sergeant	Coloma, WI	Sutfin, Paul Daniel	Specialist	Waupun, WI
Peterson, Todd Jeffrey	Sergeant First Class	Pardeeville, WI	Techlow, Robert Leonard	Specialist	Berlin, WI
Pickering, Jason Thomas	Sergeant	Fond du Lac, WI	Thelen, Benjamin Patrick	Specialist	Fond du Lac, WI
Poor, William Charles	Sergeant	Fond du Lac, WI	Tiedt, Merlin Donald	Sergeant	Columbus, WI
Posselt, Mark Oscar	Specialist	Theresa, WI	Tiegs, Robert Edward	Specialist	Mayville, WI
Quade, Alexander Ray	Sergeant	Randolph, WI	Torn, Joseph Allan	Specialist	Iron Ridge, WI
Rademann, Scott Marcus	Sergeant	Fond du Lac, WI	Trampe, Guy Welch	Specialist	Milwaukee, WI
Rath, Anthony Patrick	Private First Class	Mukwonago, WI	Troup, Richard	Specialist	Sun Prairie, WI
Reitz, Christopher William	Sergeant	Fond du Lac, WI	Van Heuklon, Scott Robert	Private First Class	Kimberly, WI
Rex, Reuben Travis Lee	Specialist	Iron Ridge, WI	Venne, Justin Matthew	Specialist	Fond du Lac, WI
Rife, Jason Michael	Specialist	Mosinee, WI	Viljevac, Arnold Paul	Sergeant	Milwaukee, WI
Ring, Michael John	Private First Class	Kaukauna, WI	Villwock, Ryan Allan	Specialist	Reeseville, WI
Robinson Adam Charles	Sergeant	Oshkosh, WI	Walker, Chad Lynn	Sergeant	Baraboo, WI
Rodewald, Corey Alan	Staff Sergeant	Whitewater, WI	Walker, Robert Alan	Staff Sergeant	Madison, WI
Rodriguez, Anthony	Specialist	Beaver Dam, WI	Wallace, Andrew Peter	Sergeant	Oshkosh, WI
Rodriguez, James Anthony	Specialist	Milwaukee, WI	Wallendal, Jason Herbert	Specialist	Fond du Lac, WI
Rooney, Justin Michael	Sergeant	Manchester, WI	Wankey, Scott Steven	Sergeant	Muskego, WI
Rosal, Matthew Alan	Specialist	Kenosha, WI	Wasmer, Steven Michael	Specialist	New Holstein, WI
Roskopf, Jeremy Scott	Specialist	Brownsville, WI	Watras, Gerard Walter	Sergeant	Fremont, WI
Sallis, Ronald David	Sergeant	Altoona, WI	Wendling, Michael Jacob	Specialist	Mayville, WI
Salverson, Thaddeus Lee	Sergeant	De Forest, WI	Wilhelms, Nathan Adam	Specialist	Fond du Lac, WI
Schack, Eric Christopher	Captain	De Pere, WI	Wilkens, Matthew Charles	Private First Class	Kiel, WI
Schmidt, Bryan James	Specialist	Hilbert, WI	Wissing, Benjamin Paul	Specialist	Ripon, WI

NAME	RANK AT TIME OF DEPLOYMENT	HOMETOWN	NAME	RANK AT TIME OF DEPLOYMENT	HOMETOWN
Wolke, Daniel Roger	Private First Class	Little Chute, WI	Lauerman, Christopher David	Specialist	Appleton, WI
Woolever, Shawn Allen	Specialist	Elkhorn, WI	Lederhaus, Daniel Herman Jr.	Specialist	Fremont, WI
Zander, Justin Reed	Specialist	Randolph, WI	Leisering, Christopher Harol	Sergeant	Fond du Lac, WI
Zuehlsdorf, Zachary Adam	Sergeant	Oshkosh, WI	Leslie, Clayton Craig	Sergeant	Pulaski, WI
			McDonald, Jonathan Mark	Specialist	Lowell, MA

Headquarters and Headquarters Company

NAME	RANK AT TIME OF DEPLOYMENT	HOMETOWN	NAME	RANK AT TIME OF DEPLOYMENT	HOMETOWN
Allen, Timothy Glenn	Sergeant	Janesville, WI	McGee, Martin Quincy	Specialist	Appleton, WI
Althoff, Kalan Lee	Staff Sergeant	Wautoma, WI	Meisenhelder, Scott Allen	Staff Sergeant	Appleton, WI
Anderson, Trevor Parker	Specialist	Green Bay, WI	Mesick, Trevor Michael	Specialist	N. Fond du Lac, WI
Aponte, David Joseph	Major	La Crosse, WI	Mooren, Adam Joseph	Specialist	Appleton, WI
Aquino, Andrew	Lieutenant Colonel	Circleville, OH	Murphy, Shawn David	Lieutenant	Sheboygan, WI
Arlen, Jody Lee	Sergeant First Class	Wausau, WI	Neta, Walter Nyle	Captain	Denmark, WI
Babl, Brett Keefe	Master Sergeant	Marinette, WI	Nowacki, Daniel Paul	Captain	Theresa, WI
Batal, Jesse Lee	Specialist	Appleton, WI	Oakley, John Thomas	Major	Appleton, WI
Biermann, Joel Thomas	Lieutenant	Watertown, WI	Obrien, Thomas Daniel	Major	Stevens Point, WI
Bolanos, Aroch	Specialist	Green Bay, WI	Orlowski, Tony James	Sergeant First Class	Watertown, WI
Buchholz, Benjamin William	Captain	Baraboo, WI	Peck, Robert Christopher	Sergeant	Neenah, WI
Carlisle, Joshua Paul	Captain	Madison, WI	Pompa, Wesley Adam	Specialist	Kaukauna, WI
Conde, Rafael	Command Sergeant Major	River Falls, WI	Potamianos, Paul Evan	Captain	Ellington, CT
Cooper, Nicholas Dominic	Specialist	Oshkosh, WI	Prokop, David Patrick	Captain	Wausau, WI
Cox, Timothy Russell	Staff Sergeant	Menominee, MI	Robbert, John Leo	Sergeant First Class	Fremont, WI
Daniels, Douglas Alan	Sergeant First Class	Eau Claire, WI	Roberts, Justin Clinton	Private	Appleton, WI
Demoulin, Jacob Justin	Specialist	Green Bay, WI	Rocheleau, Robert Lee	Specialist	Two Rivers, WI
Fenske, Jesse Michael	Sergeant	Fremont, WI	Rodriguez, Steven Jesse	Sergeant First Class	Buena Park, CA
Frei, Thomas Emery	Sergeant	La Crosse, WI	Roltgen, Timothy Richard	Sergeant	Fond du Lac, WI
Gizewski, Jeffrey Francis	Staff Sergeant	Oshkosh, WI	Rosenau, William Bird	Sergeant First Class	Neenah, WI
Goetsch, Jeremy Jay	Lieutenant	Appleton, WI	Schiermeister, John Harold II	Sergeant Major	Appleton, WI
Hahn, Donald Millard	Sergeant	Oshkosh, WI	Schuh, Thomas James	Staff Sergeant	Omro, WI
Hanssen, Jeffrey Ronald	Sergeant	Appleton, WI	Shropshire, Edward III	Sergeant	Milwaukee, WI
Haugen, Steve Albert	Staff Sergeant	New London, WI	Silva, Vital Joseph	Sergeant First Class	Green Bay, WI
Hill, Lamond Darielle	Private First Class	Neenah, WI	Sinay, Jonathan Ronald	Specialist	Palmrya, WI
Hobbs, Charles Victor	Sergeant	Eau Claire, WI	Slomski, Justin John	Private First Class	Hortonville, WI
Hoffman, Michael Scott	Sergeant	Green Bay, WI	Spangenberg, Jacob Peter	Sergeant	Menasha, WI
Hoock, Robert John	Sergeant First Class	Abbotsford, WI	Steinmetz, Douglas Richard	Staff Sergeant	Chippewa Falls, WI
Huss, Ryan Michael	Specialist	Appleton, WI	Storms, Matthew Lee	Captain	Sun Prairie, WI
Iovine, Frank Joseph	Captain	Kenosha, WI	Taves, Todd William	Lieutenant Colonel	Sussex, WI
Jagodinsky, Bruce E.	Sergeant First Class	Green Bay, WI	Thomas, Tyler Joseph	Specialist	Belmont, WI
Jeno Todd Edward Sr.	Warrant Officer	Reedsburg, WI	Torbeck, Asher Lee	Specialist	Platteville, WI
Knaack, Andrew Dale	Private First Class	Neenah, WI	Trapp, Joseph Lester	Specialist	Berlin, WI
Kohlmann, Chad Michael	Specialist	Fond du Lac, WI	Wagner, James Robert	Specialist	Black Creek, WI
Krzanowski, Darren Bernard	First Sergeant	Mosinee, WI	Wallis, Ryan Bruce	Private First Class	Montello, WI
Larson, Martin Andrew	Specialist	Muskego, WI	Wiesner, Jason Lee	Staff Sergeant	Manitowoc, WI

Index

Page numbers in italics indicate photographs.

A

B

C

D

E

Eagle River, Wisconsin, 140
educational opportunities, 140
Ehlers, Timothy, *114*
82nd Airborne Division, 27
1158th Transportation Company, 37
11th Armored Calvary Regiment, 27, 170
Ellenbecker, Dale, interview with, 57–58

e-mail and Internet, 18, 19, 70, 86, 108, 133
Employer Support of the Guard and
    Reserve, 155
EOD. *See* Explosive Ordnance Disposal teams
escort and security, 24. *See also* convoy duty
Etzel, Thomas, *154*; interview with, 46–48
Explosive Ordnance Disposal teams, 44

F

Fallujah, Iraq, 27, 170
Family Readiness Groups, 11, 80, 133, 150,
    152, 155, 157
Fenske, Jesse, *79*
56th Brigade Combat Team, 27, 170
1st Armored Division, 27
1st Battalion, 121st Field Artillery, 101,
    148–149
1st Battalion, 178th Field Artillery, 14
1st Calvary Division, 27, 170
1st Infantry Division, 27, 170
1st Marine Expeditionary Force, 27, 170

FOBs, 18, 19, 27, 170
Fond du Lac, Wisconsin, 108, *151*
Fort McCoy, Wisconsin, 86, 154, 158–161
48th Brigade Combat Team, 27, 170
42nd Infantry Division, 27, 170
forward operating bases. *See* FOBs
Fosheim, Steven, *115*, *133*, 148
4th Infantry Division, 27, 170
Fremont, Wisconsin, 140
Fritz, Jeremy, *47*, 48, 50, 154
Fritz, Steven, 50, *52*, 154; interview with, 60
Fuller, Logan, *136*

G

Gator Battalion. *See* 2nd Battalion,
    127th Infantry
Gerrits, Tyler, *36*
Gizewski, Jeffrey, *156,*
Green Bay, Wisconsin, 59, 61
Green Zone, 27, 170

Groll, Robert, 69
Guderski, Mike, interview with, 86–87
Guderski, Mitch, interview with, 86–87
Guffy, Matthew, *114*
Gulf War, 55, 75

H

I

J

K

P

Q

R

S

T

P

Q

R

S

T

Joseph Streeter